LET'S · LISTEN
TO · JESUS

Francis Asbury Publishing Company was founded in 1980 by several members of the Asbury community in Wilmore. Kentucky. Its aim was to meet the spiritual needs of that segment of the evangelical Christian public that is Wesleyan in outlook and to communicate the Wesleyan message to the larger Christian community.

In 1983 Francis Asbury Publishing Company became a part of Zondervan Publishing House. Its aim remains the spread of the Wesleyan message through the publication of popular. practical. and scholarly books.

FRANCIS ASBURY PRESS
Box 7
Wilmore. Kentucky 40390

L ET'S LISTEN
TO JESUS

Reuben R. Welch

FRANCIS ASBURY PRESS
of Zondervan Publishing House
Grand Rapids, Michigan

LET'S LISTEN TO JESUS:
REFLECTIONS ON THE FAREWELL DISCOURSE
First published under the title, *We Really Do Need to Listen,*
Copyright © 1978 by Impact Books, a division of The Benson Company.

Revised edition copyright © 1985 by The Zondervan Corporation
Grand Rapids, Michigan

FRANCIS ASBURY PRESS is an imprint of Zondervan Publishing House
1415 Lake Drive, S.E., Grand Rapids, Michigan 49506

Library of Congress Cataloging in Publication Data
Welch, Reuben.
    Let's listen to Jesus.

    Rev. ed. of: We really do need to listen. c1978.
    1. Bible. N.T. John XIII–XVII—Meditations.
I. Welch, Reuben. We really do need to listen.
II. Title.
BS2615.4.W39   1985   226'.506   85-2355
ISBN 0-310-75101-2

Edited by Joseph D. Allison
Designed by Ann Cherryman

Printed in the United States of America

85   86   87   88   89   90   /   9   8   7   6   5   4   3   2   1

To My Mother
SALLIE HARPER ROBINSON WELCH
*Who has listened with her heart
and made me want to hear.*

CONTENTS

I NTRODUCTION

It is late Thursday night of Passion Week, the last week of Jesus' earthly life. Tomorrow he will die. But on this night he is with the Eleven in the quietness of the Upper Room.

Can you see that room? It has been so carefully prepared. Yet now, at the disciples' elbows, remain only the leftovers of their broken meal. See the fragments of the broken bread? The dregs in the cup? See there, at the end of the table, the unfinished morsel Judas couldn't stomach? And there, in the corner, a bowl of cloudy water and a very dirty towel? Judas has already made his way into the black and starless night to betray his Lord. Outside the tide of hostility is rising to full hatred; tomorrow its waves will crash in on this small band of men and almost destroy them. But tonight they are together—Jesus and his disciples—and to them he opens his heart.

This book is written in the belief that we, his present-day disciples, need to listen and respond to the things Jesus shared that night. Here is the substance of a series of Bible studies conducted in churches over a period of two years, during which there was a considerable amount of "creative evolution." Neither those Bible studies nor this book can adequately cover the themes found in Jesus' words. But I earnestly hope that we can hear again some of the things Jesus shared with his disciples in that Upper Room late on the eve of his death, as recorded in John 13:31–17:26.

This beautiful section of John's Gospel has been called the Farewell Discourse or "Jesus' Last Will and Testament to His Church." These words are a rich legacy. I once read that in these comments we find everything that is most precious to our Christian heritage: every gift, every promise, every commandment, every warning, every resource that the living Christ has given to those who love him in sincerity and truth.

We are there in the Upper Room, too! So let's listen to our living Lord as he shares the gifts, commandments, and resources that we need for our Christian journey.

Jesus speaks of his departure. He speaks of the coming of the Holy Spirit. And he speaks of the quality of life to be lived within the fellowship of his followers. He looks forward to his coming again. He prays for his disciples—for their holiness, oneness, and joy. He prays that in heaven they will share with him the glory of his Father.

We should remember that the eleven men with Jesus that night represent *the church*. They have shared the covenantal meal, taken the bread of his broken body, drunk the wine of his shed blood, and participated by faith in his life, so soon to be sacrificed on Calvary. Tomorrow they will be scattered. Peter will deny him; Judas has already betrayed him; all the rest will run in fear. They are weak and human—*but they are the church!* To them Jesus opens his heart. For them he goes to die!

And we are the church. We who have participated by faith in that broken body and that poured-out blood—we who now participate by faith in the offered life of Christ through the ministry of the Holy Spirit—even in our in humanness and weakness, we are the church, the Body of Christ. I am convinced that what the Lord Jesus was saying to his church then in preparation for his departure he is saying to his church now in the duration of his departure, while he is yet present among us in the person of his Spirit.

It is important for us to realize that the words of the Farewell Discourse were written about sixty years after that night of intimate fellowship in the Upper Room. They were written after long years of the apostle John's profound meditation on the meaning of the "Christ event"—years during which he had experienced deep personal fellowship with the risen, living Christ through the ministry of his Spirit. So I can only believe that the right mental image for us, as we read the Farewell Discourse, is to visualize the risen Jesus standing in the midst of his church, opening his heart to us! From a historical point of view, the words of John 13–17 were spoken before the Crucifixion; but as the apostle John wrote these words, he saw the Jesus of the table as the risen Lord of the church. We should read these words with that understanding as well.

Mary Jo and I have been married almost forty years. There is no way for me to think of her objectively as she was when I knew her as a single woman in her late teens. All of my memories are affected by the love and fellowship, the tears and joys of these intervening years. I believe the apostle was affected by the years of intimate fellowship with his Lord in much the same way.

The point is this: As we read these words, we need to hear them not only as words spoken to the eleven disciples long ago in the Upper Room. They do not strike us as the words of a religious leader now dead. We need to listen to the words spoken by the *risen* Christ to his church, both in the first century and today. This is a living discourse of one whose words give life to all who hear and believe him.

·　·　●　·　·

The word *listen* is most significant. Christians like you and me do not take the words of Jesus as seriously as we ought. We hear them; we read them; we look at them on the printed page and recognize that we have some vague familiarity with them. But our lives are directed by them far too little. When we really hear the living Christ in the midst of his church, speaking in the power of his Spirit, we must respond and obey. Otherwise we are not genuinely listening.

Listening becomes even more important when we realize that the theology of the whole Bible is essentially a theology of the Word. That is, the Bible records how God speaks the initiating word and man responds in trustful love. God speaks in creation, in revelation, and in redemption. He speaks throughout the long history of Israel in preparation. In the fullness of time, God speaks to us in his Son, Jesus— the living Word—who is an extension of himself, and his speaking demands a response. The Bible depicts this chain of cause-and-effect where God's Word is concerned:

to listen
is to hear
is to respond
is to obey
is to believe!

When we say to our children, "You listen to me!" we really mean, "Pay attention and obey!" When Jesus said, "If any man hear my voice. . ." (Rev. 3:20), he was really saying, "If any man listens to me, he must respond . . . obey . . . believe." And in the obedience of faith, we find the way opened for sharing his life and power.

· · ● · ·

Jesus has important words for Christians like you and me. At least eight times in the Farewell Discourse he says: "These things I have spoken to you" (John 15:11). And in the great prayer of consecration he says: "I have given them the words which thou gavest me" (John 17:8). His speaking and our listening are vital to the relationship we have with the Lord. It is as if Jesus says, "You disciples—you weak, frail people who yet share my life and live in this world by my Spirit—you who are living 'between the times,' *I have words for you!* They are the words my Father gave me!"

When Jesus speaks, we need to listen!

C H A P T E R · 1

Don't
Try Harder—
Trust More

Much of what Jesus said to his friends in the Upper Room
that memorable night was in response to their questions and
interruptions. John records four of them: the first by Peter;
the second by Thomas; the third by Philip; the fourth by
Judas, "not Iscariot." I have often been grateful for those
interruptions, for some of the most significant things Jesus
ever said were in response to them. I wonder if Jesus would
have said what he did if they hadn't spoken out of their
questioning, troubled hearts that night! I wonder if we
realize that their questions are really our questions.

The Eleven are in the Upper Room with Jesus on the
night before his death. We can almost feel with them the
heaviness of the atmosphere. Profound changes are waiting
just beyond the locked door. The disciples do not understand their own sense of foreboding. They cannot fathom
the meaning of the Supper they have shared. They are
experiencing both joy and dread in the presence of their
Lord. Then Jesus begins to speak. He tells of the glory
implicit in his coming death. Then in words too weighty to
comprehend he says, "Where I am going, you cannot come"
(John 13:33).

I think I can understand the disciples' numb silence. No
questions. No response. Only silence.

Jesus goes on to talk with them of the commandment, "Love one another" (vv. 34ff.). But Peter doesn't hear. His head is spinning with the impact of the words he has just heard: "I am going . . . I am going . . . I am going." Finally we hear his outburst: *"Lord, where are you going?"*

· · ● · ·

Let us examine Jesus' answer, for I believe he led Peter to the answer by way of a detour, and I want to take that detour as well. (This is not precisely what I want to write about, but the detours of a speaker or writer are sometimes better than the main road!) "Lord," Peter said, "where are you going?"

"Where I am going you cannot follow me now; but you shall follow me afterward" (v. 36).

What a strange response! Of course Peter didn't give up his questioning with that. He persisted: "Lord, why cannot I follow you now? I will lay down my life for you."

Jesus answered, "Will you lay down your life for me? Truly, truly, I say to you, the cock will not crow, till you have denied me three times" (v. 38). Continue reading: "Let not your hearts be troubled; believe in God, believe also in me" (14:1). Notice how Jesus parries the questions:
"I am going."
　　　"Where are you going?"
"You can't follow me."
　　　"Why? I will die for you!"
"No. In fact, you will deny me."
　　　"Oh, no!"
"Oh, yes!"
　　　"No way, Lord!"
"Yes, Peter, before morning. *But let not your heart be troubled—believe!* Believe in God, believe also in me."

14

Somehow that last line does not seem to belong with the others. But that is indeed what Jesus says, and it is no accident.

We are accustomed to associating that last line with funerals. I suppose that beautiful exhortation beginning with the words, "Let not your hearts be troubled . . . ," is the classic verse of Scripture for a Christian burial. I used it myself not long ago. They are healing words for those who mourn. But Jesus did not speak them in the context of a funeral; he spoke them in the context of a failure. So they are also healing words for those who fall! In full awareness of Peter's impending failure, Jesus called him to renewed faith in the Father and in himself. Likewise he calls us in the hour of our most abject failure to keep on believing in him. Look at it this way:

Did Peter want to fail?

Of course not.

Did he intend to fail?

No.

Did he think he would fail?

No.

Did he mean what he said when he said what he said?

Yes.

BUT

Did he fail?

Yes.

Did he deny Jesus?

Yes.

Did he love Jesus?

Yes.

Then why did he deny him?

Why, indeed? I don't know the answer, but I certainly understand the question. God knows I have asked it of myself enough times! It is the question every Christian asks in the hour of failure: Why? Why? Why? But I think there is some insight for us in the astounding words of Jesus to these bewildered men.

In full awareness of the reality of our human failure, in the face of our inability to fulfill our rash promises, Jesus calls us to new faith in the Father and in himself. At the point of old failure, Jesus calls us to new faith. Could it be that failure and lack of faith are connected? Do you suppose that, at the heart of the matter, we fail because we lose faith in our Father's ability to meet all our needs?

We know that was true of our first parents in the Garden of Eden. The tragic Fall began with the insinuation of doubt: "Did God say. . . ?" At the very core of that first failure was man's loss of faith in the Father's provision for every need— man's reaching out to grasp what he no longer trusted the Father to supply. We know Adam and Eve failed because they let go of their faith in the Father. We also know that in the wilderness of his temptation, our Elder Brother over-came precisely because he never let go of his faith in his Father. The Tempter insinuated the same doubt to Jesus in the wilderness that he insinuated in the Garden: "If you are the Son of God. . . ." But our Lord never quit trusting in his Father. That trust was the source of his victory—a victory in which we may share.

I am thinking that help for our failures will come not in more self-recrimination, more self-hate, or more promises. The answer to failure in Christian living is not more struggles, more "try-harders," and more "do-betters." The answer is to be found in more faith in the Father, more faith in our Lord Jesus, more looking away from ourselves and our failures—to Jesus! That's where our strength and power really are. Someone shared this bit of verse from a minister friend:

I can't.
He never said I could!

He can.
He always said he would!

Isn't that beautiful? Like Peter, we know what it means to make rash promises and declare absolute goals. We know what it means to fail! What we need to know also is that the way out is not more promises and more unreachable goals, but more looking away from ourselves to Jesus Christ. "Believe in God, believe also in me." That is the word of Jesus himself.

· · ● · ·

Let us consider Jesus' direct answer to Peter's question, "Lord, where are you going?"
The answer given to Peter and to us all is found in John 14:2–3: "In my Father's house are many rooms; if it were not so, would I have told you that I go to prepare a place for you? And when I go and prepare a place for you, I will come again and will take you to myself, that where I am you may be also."
For too long, when I pondered this passage of Scripture, I simply concluded that Jesus was going away to get a place ready for us—that he had left *this* place and gone to *that* place to get it ready. I figured that if he could make this wonderful world in six days, heaven must be a marvelously beautiful place. But more recently I have been thinking that is not really the main point of Jesus' statement. I am discovering that the theme of "going away" is intrinsic to all of Jesus' teachings in the Gospel of John. So it is not only important to know that Jesus went way; it is important to know *how* he went and *why* he went. In fact, I am beginning to realize that the manner and meaning of his going away is the whole point of the Farewell Discourse!

Jesus went by way of ultimate encounter with our ultimate foe. He went by way of all that the Cross means, and by way of all that the Resurrection means. When death and evil had done their worst, the mighty power of God raised Jesus from the dead and exalted him in power and glory. The poured-out Spirit testifies to his conquering Lordship forever. And then we hear the promise: "I will come again" (14:3).

Take a couple of index cards and write these two promises on them to give yourself a graphic demonstration of the impact they must have had upon the disciples who first heard them. On the left-hand card write:

I GO AWAY.

On the right-hand card write these words:

I WILL COME AGAIN.

Now meditate on those two cards for a moment. Do you realize that all that you have—the whole of your human existence—rests between those two cards? Between those cards is the Cross. Between those cards Satan is ultimately defeated and your redemption is accomplished. Sin has been subdued; death has been conquered; hell has been vanquished; all the powers of evil have been overcome between those two cards. Can you see the empty tomb where the power of God raised Jesus from the dead and exalted him to the Father's right hand in glory?

I go away.

What a victory he has won!

I will come again.

What a victory he has promised!

I sometimes wonder where we are between those two great words of Jesus. Are we nearer his return than his triumph at the Cross? Many Christians think so, and maybe we are. This much is certain: We who live "between the times," between these two great words, live with great assurance. We are privileged to live in the strength of the one who has conquered sin and death, who lives among us in the fellowship of his church. And this is why Jesus can say to us weak, inadequate types, "Let not your hearts be troubled."

Jesus said, "Believe in God." Do you believe in God? He said, "Believe in me." Do you believe in him? You need to look away from your own strength and look to him, trusting him.

Throughout this passage, Jesus is saying, "I know who I am. I know what I am doing. I know where I am going. And I will come again. So it's all right." We need to hear that. In my own human weakness, I need to hear that. I need a new kind of faith based on what Jesus said. Perhaps you do, too.

I don't know where you are on your journey of faith or what your needs are as you read this book. Perhaps your dreams have crashed down around you; perhaps you are experiencing frustration and futility; perhaps you're walking in the dark and don't know what's really happening with your life. People like you and me know the meaning of failure. We know that we are not able to fulfill our own dreams and hopes by ourselves. We don't have the psychic energy or the essential motivation to be the disciples we want to be.

But, thank God, we can share the victory of our Lord Jesus Christ! We can be sure that no defeat is ultimate because Jesus' triumph is ultimate. We can live with untroubled hearts in our human situation because Jesus is in charge.

· · ● · ·

Father, our hearts say yes to the Lordship of Jesus. We bow before you in our human frailty, confessing that we have often failed, tried harder, promised more—and failed again because we trusted ourselves alone.

But now your Son has come. He has triumphed over everything that threatens to defeat us. So we look away from ourselves to Jesus Christ.

Lord Jesus, we thank you that we can live with untroubled hearts because you are Lord! How we need untroubled hearts! So we look to you in trust and with genuine thanks. Amen.

CHAPTER · 2

I Am the Road Under Your Feet

Jesus' response to Peter's question led inevitably to another interruption, this time by Thomas. Jesus had said, "I am going to the Father." Thomas now asked, in effect, "How can we get there?" And Jesus answered his question with the wondrous statement: "I am the way, and the truth, and the life; no one comes to the Father, but by me" (John 14:6).

Thus we have Jesus' response to one of the most significant questions a person ever can ask: "How can we know the way?" Jesus says simply, "I am the way. . . ."

Jesus is the true way to the Father because (1) he reveals to us the truth about the Father and (2) he shares with us the life of the Father. The truth he reveals is the truth that Jesus himself is; the life that he gives is Jesus' own life. So this is one of the simplest yet most profound truths that we can hear from Jesus' lips.

Jesus' statement, "No one comes to the Father, but by me," is not an arbitrary negative. It does not imply snobbishness or exclusivism. Jesus does not selfishly lock up all other doors to God and throw away the keys! Only God can open up the way to God; and that is what Jesus does in this simple statement.

We can't search for God and find him for ourselves over the brow of some hill or around the corner of the next

21

building we pass. We do not suddenly come upon God and say, "Oh, *there* you are!" God makes himself known to us. So the way to God is the way *of* God. He shows us the way; and the way is Jesus.

· · ● · ·

I hope you will forgive another little detour concerning the word, *way.* Stop reading for a moment and let your mind run through the Bible, lifting out verses that you can remember that have the word *way* in them. Here are several that I have been thinking of:

Teach me thy *way,* O LORD;
and lead me on a level path
because of my enemies (Ps. 27:11).

Jesus said, "I am the way."

Commit your *way* to the Lord;
trust in him, and he will act (Ps. 37:5).

Jesus said, "I am the way."

Your ears shall hear a word
behind you, saying,
"This is the *way,* walk in it" (Isa. 30:21).

Jesus said, "I am the way."

We have turned every one
to his own *way* (Isa. 53:6).

Jesus said, "I am the way."

I wonder if Jesus was remembering verses like these when he said, "I am the way." I think this verse from Proverbs is also significant:

> There is a *way*
> which seems right to a man,
> but its end is the *way* to death (14:12).

I think Jesus was surely thinking of this when he answered Thomas. The way of man is the way of his own choosing— *and it is the way of death!* Jesus alone is the true Way, and he leads to life.

· · ● · ·

What do we really mean when we say Jesus is "the Way"? We know that he points the way for us; but he is more than a way-pointer. He doesn't simply give us directions and disciplines for our journey to God. He is more than the gurus of Oriental religions who share the secrets of their enlightenment and point the way to some god at the top of a mountain. He is more than "the way to God" in the sense that Shakespeare is "the way" to poetry or Saint Francis is "the way" to the serving life.

We are closer to the truth when we say that *Jesus goes with us on the way; he is our companion on the journey.* At this point I'm thinking of an old gospel song:

> He will give me grace and glory,
> And go with me, with me all the way.
> — E.W. Blandy

That sentiment gives us a better insight into the true sense in which Jesus is our way to God.

Perhaps the adherents to Oriental religions aren't the only ones who put God on top of a mountain and view him as a goal to be achieved or an end to be realized. We Christians are tempted to think of him that way too. I remember that when Mary Jo and I were pastoring a church in Honolulu, a young mother said, "Reverend, when I get good enough, I'm going to become a Christian and join your church." And I wonder if someone who's reading these words is saying, "When I get strong enough, I'm going to enter the victorious life." or, "When I get good enough, I'm going to be the Christian I want to be." or, "When I'm what I ought to be, then I will feel worthy to come to God." If so, Jesus has a word for you right here! The good news is that the God of the mountain comes all the way down to where you are and says, "Let me walk with you." There is no reaching up to find God; there is no uphill journey to meet God. He is not sitting high above the clouds calling out, "Come on up! It's beautiful up here!" But in infinite, caring love he comes to where you are right now and becomes the loving, strengthening companion on your journey.

But we mean much more than this when we say that Jesus "is the way." He is more than the way-pointer, more than our companion on the way; *he is the way!*

While teaching Greek, I discovered that the New Testament word translated *way* is also the Greek word for *road*. This fact has given me an entirely new understanding of what Jesus said about himself. We have made *way* a stained-glass word; we pronounce it in hushed tones, as if it belongs in a church. Let's put a stained-glass window in the church. Can you see it? There is the crown, the flames, the dove. There are the beautiful muted colors and symbols. And woven throughout is the banner in Old English letters:

I AM THE WAY, THE TRUTH, AND THE LIFE.

Somehow the word *road* doesn't fit that window very well. It belongs where our lives are lived. It reminds us of the paths we walk, the sidewalks of our towns and cities, the streets and highways of our busy world. Yet I believe that Jesus meant the word *way* to be understood precisely where our real lives are lived.

Someone has explained it this way: Jesus did not say, "At the end of the road, there you will find me." He said, "I am the very road under your feet!" In other words, wherever you are, Jesus is there. If you are on the spiritual mountaintop, he is there; if you are in the valley, he is there; if you are in the pit, he is there. We do not have to come where he is. He is where we are. We do not have to reach up to grasp him. He has reached down to grasp us.

As you read these words, do you suspect that God is so far away that you can never find him? that your life is too messed up to be set in order? that your patterns of failure are too deeply set to be broken? that your entanglements are too complex to be straightened out? that your goal is so distant there is no use to try? *Don't believe it! That is the Devil's lie!*

Regardless of how you feel or how complicated the problems of your life, you can be sure that Jesus is where you are right now—feeling what you feel, thinking what you think, experiencing what you experience—where you are, as you are right now! Saint Augustine seemed to understand this when he spoke the words that all of us need to hear:

> I do not say to thee, Seek a way.
> The Way himself has come to thee;
> arise and walk!

· · ● · ·

Lord Jesus, we try so hard to get where you are, though you have come to us. I accept the fact that you are the road under my feet. I let my weight settle down upon you, knowing that I can walk confidently if you are my road and my strength. I have hope if you are where I am. I thank you for being here, Jesus, my Way and my Road. Amen.

CHAPTER · 3

See for Yourself

The more I study these interruptions by the disciples, the more I am convinced they are not recorded by accident; nor did they occur by accident. I am convinced the disciples raised these comments and questions on their last night with Jesus as a result of divine ordering. They ask *the* great questions of the human race. And Jesus responds to them with *the* great answers!

First: "Where are you going?"

Then: "How can we know the way?"

Now Philip's probing request: "Lord, show us the Father, and we shall be satisfied" (John 14:8).

Philip was a good Jew and had heard about God all his life. From a child he had been taught the Scriptures. He had a God-language, understood God-talk, and used God-words. Yet some hunger within him, dormant through those years of rote religion, was called to life by the presence and ministry of Jesus. So out of the depths of his soul came this haunting question, "What is God like?" Though Philip had heard about God all his life, he was still unsatisfied because he did not know God as his Father!

There is a striking difference between knowing about God and knowing God. We may know the right God-words yet not experience God. Only in Jesus, the Son of God, can we truly know God the Father. "Show us the Father, and we shall be satisfied," Philip cried. How true! If only we knew God as our Father, as Jesus knew him, we would be satisfied indeed.

For Jesus the Fatherhood of God was no dull and dusty theological fact. The Fatherhood of God was Jesus' life, breath, and soul. He lived in obedience to his Father. He fully depended upon his Father. He spoke with the authority of his Father. He died in the will of his Father. He was raised by the power of his Father! Such a life was sure to attract the attention of one like Philip, who knew the form but not the reality of a godly life.

I wonder if I am writing to someone who, like Philip, has known about God for years without really knowing him as Father. I wonder if behind the familiar God-words you have a gnawing desire to know the Father. That desire takes the shape of dissatisfaction and lack of fulfillment which haunts your days and nags your times of devotion. How sad to know the right God-language without knowing God himself; yet is that where you find yourself right now?

The joy, satisfaction, authority, and confidence that you crave are intimately related to having real fellowship with God *as your Father.* I believe that beneath Philip's simple request, "show us the Father," was a hungering desire to know the fullness of spiritual life. His question is the fundamental one for each of us. Our most pressing question is not, "Does God exist?" Of course we believe that he exists. Oh, yes, we have our moments of doubting and wondering; we have our perplexing questions when we face the mystery of evil and the sometimes absurd, irrational events of our lives. But these times of perplexity are not permanent. We come back to our moorings. Our faith is well-anchored in the reality of God.

But we do have a problem about God, and I think it is a very serious one. Our question is, "What is God like?" And I cannot really convey to you how important that question is!

I am not so naive as to assume that all of us have the same quality of religious understanding. Many of us, brought up in the teaching of the church, have some ideas about God that are positively weird. If I could, I would give you a 3x5 card with this question at the top: WHAT IS GOD LIKE? I would ask you to take a minute or two to answer that question in twenty-five well-chosen words. (Since we are talking about it, why don't you go ahead and do it?) I think the way you answer the question on that card lays the foundation for the way you answer every other important question of your life. Let me illustrate what I mean with a couple of episodes taken from my own life. I mention them because they have become symbols of my life, and in other forms have been repeated over and over.

One day a troubled girl came to see me in my office at school. She dropped into a chair and, on the verge of tears, she exclaimed, "I don't like me!"

We began to talk about her feelings and soon the conversation drifted around to the subject of God. "Sometimes I think God is like my grandmother," she said. "And that's good because my grandmother is neat! But most of the time I think God is like my grandfather."

"That's *not* so neat?"

"No! He comes from a long line of Prussian army officers."

When she said that, a little light went on in my head. Depression, frustration, low self-esteem, guilt, unhappiness—she knew them all. And underneath them all was a very bad image of God. Her God was sometimes like her gentle, loving grandmother; but mostly he was like her strict, stern, disciplinarian grandfather.

Do you see how faith, trust, and obedience are affected by our understanding of God? Martin Luther once had a difficult time with the Lord's Prayer. When he said the words, "Our Father," he thought of his own father. . .and then I guess he thought of the Devil, because he didn't want to pray anymore! I wonder how many other Christians have that problem.

Here is another episode that illustrates the importance of our understanding of God. A long time ago I was preaching at a church in Globe, Arizona when I met a woman whose husband had left her and their son, about four or five years old. After church service one evening, this lady began to talk with me about her doubts and fears, her trouble and pain, her loneliness and heartache, and. . .her questions about God. She wondered, "Does God really care?"

After listening for a while, I asked, "Have you ever gone out under the stars or knelt down by your bed and told God all the things you're telling me?"

I will never forget her answer: "Oh, no! There are some things you just don't tell God!"

Really?

A few months later I saw her at a camp meeting. On the path between the tabernacle and the cabins we talked. The camp-meeting preacher had been laying on us some of the great words:

> *Yield* to God.
> *Obey* God.
> *Surrender* to God.
> *Give* everything to God.

And she was having problems with this. She said, "I can give myself to God, but I can't give my little boy to God. God can do whatever he wants with me. But I won't give my boy to him."

I probably picked up where the preacher had left off:

> *Love* God.
> *Trust* God.
> *Surrender* to God.
> *Yield everything* to God.
> *Give your boy to God.* . . .

"But I can't!"

"Why not?"

"Because I'm afraid God will take him!"

That was when another light went on in my head! I was pouring out to this lady the good words, the big words, the life-changing words. And they were all sounding like the bad words, the hard words, the dark words, the impossible words *because her mental image of God was bad.* I read somewhere that a false mental image of God is just as bad as a false *metal* image of God. I believe that.

Let us go back and listen to those two persons talking on the campground pathway:

"Give everything to God. Give your boy to God."

"I can't."

"You must."

"I cannot."

"Why not?"

"I'm afraid God will take him!"

Can you see that the entire conversation was conditioned (on both sides) by our mental images of God? One person saw God as the loving Father to whom all things great and small could be entrusted. The other saw him as an unfeeling, mechanical monster whose cold, steel paw was programmed to scoop up the precious gift she was commanded to offer. I think that if I felt that way about God, I wouldn't trust him either!

If we had moved that conversation off the campground and into the church sanctuary and surrounded it with sentimental music, sweet organ sounds, and songs of dedication, that mother might have burst into tears and made some act of response or said the expected words. But nothing really would have been changed. Her image of God would have remained the same.

I must admit that we preachers don't help people with their image of God in times of death or other kinds of loss. Ever hear words like these at the funeral of a child?

God saw this little rosebud one day—so perfect, so fragrant—and he wanted it for his heavenly garden. So he reached down and plucked it and planted it to bloom in heaven. . . .

How awful! How pagan! God is not a sovereign gardener who sees, desires, and snatches precious children in death! Yet we have perpetuated that horrible notion with our sentimental soliloquies at the graveside. I believe that at every moment of life, but especially the traumatic moments, we should convey the truth that we can safely trust God and give everything to him.

Well, I have said all of this to explain that the twenty-five well-chosen words you have written on the 3x5 card are supremely important to the whole of your life. What you think of God really matters.

· · ● · ·

What *is* God like? Jesus said, "He who has seen me has seen the Father." God is like Jesus!

Now would you turn your card over and put a second question on the other side? The first question was, "What is God like?" The second question is, "Where did you get that idea?" Not only is it important to know what we think of God; it is also important to know where we got our thoughts of him.

We gather up data that determines our most fundamental decisions of life in an offhand, casual, almost accidental matter. How often we have heard people in prayer groups, Bible study groups, and Sunday school classes begin to make some profound conclusions with words such as: "I've always thought that. . ." or, "We were always taught in our home that. . ." or, "I once heard a preacher say. . . ." And here is the classic: "Isn't there a verse in the Bible somewhere that says something about. . . ?"

Unfortunately, some of our most significant concepts have been collected at random. Could it be that our ideas of God grow that way?

Each of us seems to have a kind of spiritual Polaroid camera with which we take snapshots of certain events in our lives, and thereby gather up our ideas of God. When we lived in Pasadena, we had a family room with a bulletin board on one wall. We tacked all sorts of photos on that board: the cat and dog sleeping together like friends, Rob's baseball team, Susan's choir pictures, snaps from our last vacation, an invitation to a wedding. All of these formed a friendly collage of family "stuff." When we moved to our house in San Diego, we gave the whole thing a bit more class; we selected some of the better family pictures, framed them, and hung them on the wall in style. The friendly "junk stuff" ended up stuck on the refrigerator with magnets! Yet I think the informal collection reveals as much about us as the collection that is on display for visitors. I have been thinking that somewhere in the back room of the soul there must be a bulletin board labeled, "GOD," and through the years we have collected various impressions and tacked them to the board in what has become a collage of our God-image. A tragedy happens in a godly family. . . .

Click!

Why did God let that happen? A bad picture goes on the board. We read the Old Testament story of Moses and Pharaoh, get the idea that God hardened Pharaoh's heart and then turned around and clobbered him for it. . . .

Click!

What's going on here? Another negative picture. A father beats his children. . . .

Click!

Someone in the church gets sick and everyone prays, but the sufferer dies. . . .

    Click!

Someone in the church gets sick. Everyone prays and the person recovers. . . .

    Click!

That's better! Someone has a remarkable conversion experience. . . .

    Click! Click!

That's much better! A church member starts tithing and gets rich. . . .

    All right, Lord!

And we use a whole roll of film!

Love God. Trust God. Obey God. Give everything to God. . . . The collage is balancing out, and the big words are sounding better. Do you see what is happening? We are gathering up data from the experiences of our lives and constructing our own ideas of God out of them. If our lives are good—our God is good. If our lives are bad—our God is bad. How tragic!

You surely know someone who has said something like this: "Don't talk to me about God! My mother got sick and I prayed for her to be healed and she died anyway. So don't talk to me about God!"

On the other hand, you probably know people whose view of God is shallow and sentimental: "He is so wonderful because he answers all my prayers and solves all my problems and gives me so much happiness." What do those people say when trouble comes?

What we think of God makes a tremendous difference in our lives. Where we get our ideas of God makes a tremendous difference too. We can gather up data and develop our own image of God, or we can allow God to reveal himself in a self-portrait—his Son, Jesus Christ.

What sort of pictures do you have on your board? Will you let the Holy Spirit clear them away and replace them with a picture of the New Testament Jesus? Or do you prefer to hold onto childhood images and outdated mementoes of God? Those images can be so false and distorted that it is impossible to see God as he wishes to be seen, in the person of Jesus Christ. Everything, in the final analysis, hangs on this peg: *God is like Jesus.*

I guess we really don't need twenty-five words to answer the questions on our 3x5 card. We only need one. What is God like? *Jesus.* Where did we get that idea? *Jesus.*

I am hearing again the big words of the Christian faith: Love God. Obey God. Trust God. Give everything to God. If God is like Jesus, then these are truly good words, life-transforming words. To them and to the Christlike God my heart is saying, "Yes! Yes! Yes!"

· · ● · ·

Yes, Jesus, yes. If God is like you, my heart says yes! But it is hard to let go of old ideas, feelings, and images. Give me the grace to bring them all to you. Let your Holy Spirit cleanse and replace the false God-images I have carried so long. Let him fill my heart and mind with the vision of yourself. Amen.

CHAPTER · 4

I Am Real

Judas' question brings all the realities exposed by the previous questions into the realm of personal experience. Judas asks Jesus, "How is it that you will manifest yourself to us, and not to the world?" (John 14:22). Or to phrase the question in the third person, "How does Jesus become real to us?"

Peter wanted to know where his Lord was going. Thomas wanted to know how to get there. Philip wanted to know what God is like. And Jesus' answers to these three questions express the great central truths of the gospel:

Jesus is Lord.

He is the way to the Father.

He is the revelation of the Father.

But Judas' question remains: "How does Jesus become real to us?" We may believe the great truths without internalizing them; we may hold great realities that are not real to us; and we may know *about* Jesus without knowing him. How do we come to know God? How does he become real to us?

This question meets us wherever we are on our journey. Some of us have heard the holy doctrines of the church all our lives, but they have never come alive within us. Some of us have really come to know Christ, but we have not allowed his lordship to enter certain hidden areas of our lives; we have posted "Keep Out" signs there and forbidden him to enter. Some of us have enjoyed thrilling religious experiences, but the truths we discovered there have not made much difference in our behavior; in other words, no one could tell we had an experience of Christ by looking at our lives. No matter where we are or where we have been, we could ask Judas' question: "Lord, how will you manifest yourself *to us?*" And here is Jesus' reply: "If a man loves me, he will keep my word, and my Father will love him, and we will come to him and make our home with him" (John 14:23).

Did Jesus say, "If a man loves me, he will have a thrilling emotional experience"? Or, "If a man loves me, he will be able to perform some great spiritual feat"? No. But notice very carefully what Jesus *did* say.

I am hesitant to write about this point because I believe in the validity of personal experience. But I must write about the danger of depending too much upon experience. I believe that experiences can be removed from the truth, and the sensuous atmosphere of our society has tipped the scales in favor of emotionalism in religious experience as well as in every other experience of life.

We do live in a sensual age. We are conditioned by the advertising media to want "good vibes," pleasant feelings, and exciting sensations. Salespersons use touch, taste, sound, smell, sight, and erotic stimuli as tools in their selling game. Everything from tractors to toothpaste, soup to sewing machines are offered to us for sensuous reasons. We are kidding ourselves if we pretend that we are not affected by all of this.

Not only is ours a sensuous age physically and materially; it is a sensuous age spiritually. There is a kind of "spiritual sensualism," and many of us evangelical Christians have slipped into it. We want the Holy Spirit to lift us up like the tide and set us down on the shore of heaven, in some fantastic mystical experience. We want to be sky blue and red hot. We want to be ready to go and meet our Maker on a moment's notice—no doubts and no questions, just praise the Lord!

"How are you?"

"Fantastic!" (We can't even say "Fine" anymore. We want a gospel experience that brings us emotional joy and lots of "fantastic.")

I don't mind saying "we," because I enjoy having chills up and down my spine as much as you do. I like to feel blessed, to get all charged up, and to float around on Cloud Nine. But in Jesus' word to Judas I hear that we don't need a newer, deeper, more fantastic experience. Jesus says that what we really need is genuine, careful, deliberate obedience to what we have already experienced.

· · ● · ·

When we focus on the idea of *obedience,* we're not talking about doing things we can't understand or can't do. We're not talking about the words of Jesus that are too much for us. What bothers us as Christians are Jesus' words that are understandable and do-able. What disturbs us is the difficulty of letting Jesus' words come down into our daily conversation, into our daily patterns of thought, response, and decision.

Mary Jo and I have been married a long time now, and everyone knows that in a good long-term relationship there must be some ground rules. Well, I am proud to announce that we have established the ground rules at our house: *I make the big decisions and she makes the little ones.*

I make the big decisions: How are we going to handle the nuclear arms race? How are we going to reestablish the moral strength of our government? What are we going to do about cleaning up toxic waste sites?

Mary Jo makes the little decisions: Where are we going to live? How are we going to spend our money? What am I going to do with my time today? This division of labor is not so strange for Christians; in fact, we do it all the time. We let God make the big decisions and we make the little ones!

But we must let the words of Jesus seep into the attitudes, responses, and decisions of daily life. In this process, our heavenly Father makes himself known to us in loving intimacy. We can know God the Father both in precept and in person; and the key to this knowledge is *obedience*. This greatest of all knowing is ours, not by virtue of some marvelous spiritual achievement or some fantastic spiritual experience, but by simple, loving obedience.

· · ● · ·

A delightful promise is contained in Jesus' answer to Judas. Jesus places our knowledge of God in the context of love and home, saying, "My Father will love him, and we will come to him and make our home with him" (v. 23). This promise continues the wonderful harmony between God and home portrayed throughout the Bible.

When God created man, he did not set him in isolation but in community, in a family. God promised Abraham a family, and Abraham became the father of a great nation. God revealed himself to Hosea as the forgiving husband and father of his wayward people. God sent his Son, Jesus Christ, to gather us into the family of God, making all of us brothers and sisters in him, providing us a beautiful earthly home while making us ready for a home in heaven. Throughout

Scripture our knowledge of God is inextricably related to our experience of home and family.

Remember Jesus' promise from Revelation: "Behold, I stand at the door and knock; if any one hears my voice and opens the door, I will come in to him and eat with him, and he with me" (3:20). People of all places and all times have found that coming to Jesus is like coming home. It's an experience that feels warm, familiar, and right because of our very purpose for living: We were created to be with him.

Is Jesus real to you? You have a place where you can start to know him in your own life: *Begin to obey* simply and honestly the words of Jesus that you understand—the words that speak clearly to your situation and your needs. I believe that if you do that, you will discover Jesus' promise is true; he will come home with you.

· · ● · ·

O Jesus, you have made God clear to us. You have brought him near to us and made him dear to us. For that we thank you.

We want to be at home with you. Teach us how we can begin to be in fellowship with you, through simple obedience to what you have said. Lord, help us to listen. Amen.

CHAPTER · 5

Don't Quit Now

The fifteenth chapter of John has been called the "Discourse on Relationships." In the first paragraph Jesus talks to his disciples about their relationship with him (vv. 1–11); in the second he talks about their relationship with each other (vv. 12–17); and in the third he talks about their relationship with the hostile world (vv. 18–27). In this book I am especially concerned with the first paragraph; what does Jesus say about our relationship with him? What does that relationship mean in our daily lives?

Here are some of his words: "I am the true vine, and my Father is the vinedresser. Every branch of mine that bears no fruit, he takes away, and every branch that does bear fruit he prunes, that it may bear more fruit. I am the vine, you are the branches. He who abides in me, and I in him, he it is that bears much fruit, for apart from me you can do nothing" (vv. 1–5).

The *vine* had been a symbol of Israel's religious heritage for centuries. Israel pictured herself as the vineyard of the Lord or a noble vine of God's own planting. Prophets referred to Israel as the tender vine that God had removed from Egypt and transplanted to the land of Canaan with the intention that it take root, grow, and flourish, covering the world with his grace and blessing.

But here is the sad thing: Israel, the vine of God's planting, never became the missionary people through whom God could bless the world. It never grew over the wall! So Isaiah declared that Israel had become a vineyard run wild. Jeremiah complained that Israel was a degenerate plant. Hosea mourned that Israel was a barren vine. Perhaps it is out of this background that Jesus proclaimed, "I am the true vine." His roots are in the very heart of God. His love, grace, and healing reach out to cover the world. As the true vine, Jesus is the bearer of the very life of God to every human being.

But I think the most astonishing part of Jesus' statement is the next line: "You are the branches." He is God's vine; we are the branches. What a beautiful metaphor! Jesus uses the relationship he has with the Father as an analogy of our relationship with each other and with Jesus himself. What an awesome truth that is! Jesus explains more specifically what he means in verses 9 and 10:

> As the Father has loved me, so have I loved you; abide in my love. If you keep my commandments, you will abide in my love, just as I have kept my Father's commandments and abide in his love.

As the Father's love is toward the Son, so the Son's love is toward us. As the Son abides through obedience, so we abide in the Son's love through obedience. We would never have had the audacity to use the intimate relationship of God the Father and Christ the Son as an analogy for our own relationship with the Lord Jesus. But Jesus did!

· · ● · ·

As we read these verses, we are struck by the beautiful imagery of the vine and branches. But the fundamental result of the vine-branch relationship is *fruitfulness*. Verse 2 speaks of vines that "bear no fruit," "do bear fruit," and "bear more fruit." Verses 5 and 8 exhort us to "bear much fruit." Obviously, the concept of fruit-bearing is central to what Jesus is saying here.

Perhaps because I grew up on a farm, the idea of fruit-bearing is quite appealing to me. I want to be a fruitful person for God. Yet I am beginning to realize that I don't understand a great deal about the significance of bearing fruit for him. How can I define spiritual fruit-bearing?

Galatians 5:22 describes the "fruit of the Spirit" in terms of love, joy, peace, patience, kindness, goodness, faithfulness, gentleness, and self-control. Paul speaks of "bearing fruit in every good work and increasing in the knowledge of God" (Col. 1:10) and of being "filled with the fruits of righteousness which come through Jesus Christ" (Phil. 1:11). These verses suggest that spiritual fruit-bearing means *reproduction in kind*—as when orange trees reproduce oranges, people reproduce people, or Christians reproduce Christians.

However we define it—whether spiritual fruit-bearing implies growth in grace, productivity, maturity, joy, abundance, or whatever else—I want it. I imagine that you do too.

· · ● · ·

We know that Jesus was a fruitful person. He was greatly concerned for the fruitfulness of the infant body of believers to whom he poured out his heart in the Upper Room that night. So in this paragraph Jesus speaks of several things that are inevitably related to fruit-bearing, things that deserve our careful attention if we wish to bear fruit for the Lord.

For one thing, Jesus says that fruit-bearing involves submission to the pruning process. When I grew up in central California on a citrus ranch, I did not learn much about pruning. But I knew that we pruned the citrus trees for two reasons: to cut away the dead branches that had been frostbitten the previous winter and to cut out the suckers that looked lush and green but drained precious life from the trees, preventing them from producing any fruit. When we moved to Pasadena, we began raising grapevines. There the pruning was disastrous—it meant no fruit the next year and very little fruit the following year. But we pruned grapes for the same reasons we pruned the citrus trees: Fruit can be produced on new growth, while old branches hinder the flow of life.

The things we let go are no less significant for our fruitfulness than the things we keep.

A college professor told me about a famous ichthyologist who knew the names of thousands of fish. But he reached a point in his life when he discovered that if he learned the name of a new student, he forgot the name of an old fish! I think I understand that problem. Most of the time my garage is in that condition—if anything new comes in, something old has got to go out! The parting can be painful, but garage sales have become a normal part of my life.

I remember the day we sold our tandem bike. I bought it, thinking that Mary Jo and I would have fun on it and stay healthy with it. But we rode that bike just enough to get sore! Our legs hurt too much to stand; our bottoms hurt too much to sit. So I hung it in the garage with nylon ropes and pulleys. There it collected dust and seldom came down. I grieved to give it up, but it really needed to go. Like other things, the tandem bike not only cluttered the garage, it cluttered our minds and used up psychic energy. Every time we saw that bike, though no words were spoken, our thoughts and emotions were stirred: *Are we going to ride it? When? Where? Why? Why not?* Despite those defensive thoughts and conflicting emotions, the bike really needed to go.

What a small thing that was. Yet the bike symbolizes all the other things—boats, trailers, tools, clothes, cars—that we keep hanging onto. We keep spending, gathering up, holding on until we are too busy to use our gathered things or we get another job to pay for them! We pick up attitudes, habits, and relationships that draw off our energies and sap our strength. Then we wonder why we aren't joyful, growing, and productive.

The pruning process makes me think too about things we read, watch on TV, and think about. I wonder if some folks ever have any thoughts besides thoughts of sports, making money, or buying things. The same might be said about our spiritual thoughts—our ideas of God, of Scripture, and of the church. How many of us have minds filled with childhood's leftover notions? How many of us have hearts cluttered with outgrown hurts and obsolete perceptions? And the clutter grows until there is no room for fresh understandings and attitudes, no room for new fruit.

You know, we ought to have a spiritual garage sale!

The Greek word for *prune* in verse 2 is translated *clean* in verse 3; it is the root of our English word, *catharsis*. John 15 teaches us that our pruning (and cleansing) comes through obedience to the words of Jesus.

Jesus' pruning process came about through obedience to his Father's word. Think of all the things Jesus could have done, and didn't. Think of all the things he could have had, and didn't. But how much he accomplished because he didn't try to do everything! How much he really had because he didn't try to possess so much!

You and I could be likewise cleansed and liberated if we obeyed the words of Jesus. We need to back away, take a good look at our lifestyle, and ask, "Jesus, do you have anything to say about all this?" Every one of us has times when we hunger for a change in ourselves and our style of life. All of us have the feeling, sooner or later, that there must be a better way. I believe God gives us these times of discontent to woo us into listening quietly and obediently to the words of Jesus. I believe they are times when he invites us to yield to the pruning of Jesus.

Does the Word expose a restricting habit in your life? Does the Word point out a destructive relationship that ought to be broken off? Does it reveal a lot of clutter or barrenness in your life? What does the word of Jesus find in your life today?

Perhaps a hobby has become your master, a possession has become a passion, or a recreation has become nonrecreative. If so, listen to the words of Jesus. Obey his words and you will experience the pruning that brings true fruitfulness. I'm realizing anew, even as I write these words, that although we can rationalize almost anything we can afford or really want, the words of Jesus lead us into the joyous pain of self-surrender. And that kind of obedience brings abundance.

· · ● · ·

Hear another important word from Jesus as he challenges us not only about pruning but about praying: "If you abide in me, and my words abide in you, *ask whatever you will,* and it shall be done for you. By this my Father is glorified, so that you bear much fruit, and so prove to be my disciples" (vv. 7–8, italics mine).

I wish I knew how to understand fully the words, "Ask whatever you will, and it will be done for you." The man who spoke these words did not get the answer he wanted to the most agonizing prayer he ever prayed: "My Father, if it be possible, let this cup pass from me" (Matt. 26:39). Yet Jesus lived in a confident, prayerful relationship with his heavenly Father and advised us to have that same kind of attitude. He tells us to ask confidently, trustfully for whatever we want. That is not the final word about prayer, but it certainly is the first word. *We are told to ask for whatever we want.*

Sometimes we ask hesitantly, "Is it all right to ask God for. . . ?" "Is it all right to pray about. . . ?" Yet there is nothing about which we cannot pray. Whatever we are thinking, we had best be praying! Things refined or gross, clean or sordid, light or dark—whatever we think, whatever we desire, whatever we feel should be opened up to God. Only in this way can our relationship with the Father be like our Lord's relationship, utterly honest and open.

I am sure you have heard a couple say, "We share everything. There are no secrets between us. Our relationship is absolutely open!" Well, don't believe it totally. There is no way we can be completely open with another human being; we have too much to lose. But everything—everything—can be opened up to God.

Think of it this way: We have desires that are worthy or unworthy, trivial or profound, beautiful or ugly, spiritual or materialistic. But if we place a filter over them so that we express only certain desires in prayer, then we are living at two levels.

Visualize the thoughts and desires deep within you. You don't know whether you should pray about them, but they are there. They have to do with your home, your work, your school life, how you are being treated, how you are being loved or not loved, whether you are being affirmed as a human being or not affirmed. Imagine all of these desires living in the cage of your soul. What if you put a grid over them and only let the "worthy" ones out of the cage in the form of prayer? What will happen to the cage full of real thoughts and feelings that are unshared, unopened, and unprayed?

God calls us to take away the grid, to uncover the cage,

and to let it all out in prayer. Are they unworthy desires? *Lord, reveal their unworthiness.* Are they selfish ambitions? *Lord, what do you say?*

I believe that only as all of our desires are opened to God can they be cleansed so that change, growth, and fruitfulness can begin. If we pray only our holy prayers, our unholy thoughts remain unholy still, pacing the cage and feeding on our fantasies and daydreams. They may grow strong enough to break out of the cage, wrecking havoc and causing a "holy" person to do unholy things. We wonder, *How can that be?* I believe it is because the unacceptable was not truly opened up to God for his cleansing and healing grace.

I am hearing the words of Jesus once again: "If you abide in me and my words abide in you, ask whatever you will. . . ." If we will pray, he will filter. That is part of God's way to fruitfulness.

· · ● · ·

Let us consider one more word related to fruit-bearing; it is the word *abide.* Three times it is used in this short paragraph: "Abide in me and I in you" (v. 4). "Abide in me and my words abide in you" (v. 7). "Abide in my love" (v. 9).

In an earlier chapter I said that the word *way* was a stained-glass word. *Abide* is that kind of word, too. We feel it belongs on the banner printed in Old English, stretching across the Gothic window. Looks beautiful with the light shining through, doesn't it?

But the word *abide* doesn't really belong there because it has a very practical, everyday meaning. It means *stay* as in the command "Sit!" If instead of a cathedral we were to build a Jesus-People-House-Church, we would replace the stained-glass window with the familiar poster that shows a cat hanging on a clothesline with the caption, "Hang in there, Baby!" That is what the word *abide* really means.

Our Lord ties abiding together with fruit-bearing in a way that gives hope to us all.

What is the difference between those who begin the Christian journey and quit, and those who begin and don't quit? Ever wonder about that? My guess is that if all the people who had come through the front door of your church in the last ten years had stayed (and none had left through the back door), your church would be far larger than it is today.

Some folks come into the Christian faith to stay and grow. Some begin with a lot of sparkle and pizazz, then drop out. I've wondered why. Are some people religious by nature, while others are irreligious?

I used to think I could spot religious people; then I attended a general assembly of our church and found I could only tell the religious people by their delegate badges. (Well, that's almost true!) I used to think I could identify the preacher types; then I went to a preachers' meeting and saw every personality type under the sun! (Some folks think there is a preacher's *wife* type! I remember a ministerial student who was in love with this wonderful girl but worried that she didn't fit the image of a minister's wife. I wanted to hit him over the head with some large, blunt object to get his attention and then yell, "No! No! No!")

I have concluded that people don't leave the church or stay in the church because of personality type.

Do you suppose some people begin the Christian journey and hang in there because, by some providence of God, they have been spared the heavy sorrows of life? Do you think they stay because "the grass is greener over here," and they haven't had to struggle with pain and doubt and tragedy? Of course not. God's people experience such things.

So what keeps some Christians staying in the family of

God, abiding? I think I have finally found the answer: The folks who begin and keep on going are the ones who don't quit!

The secret of a fruitful life is abiding, staying with the Lord, hanging in there. "Abide in me. . . . Abide in my love. . . . Abide in me and my words abide in you." The wonder of it all is that spiritual fruitfulness is not for the special, virile few. It comes to any of us in the same way it came to Jesus. He submitted to his Father's pruning; he opened his whole heart to his Father in prayer; and he didn't quit!

As I write these words, I am beginning to feel that there is hope for me too!

· · ● · ·

Lord, we thank you that there is hope for us. We want so much to be fruitful. We need so much help in our praying and obeying. Remind us again that we belong to you and share your very life, as branches share the life of the vine. Help us stay in your love and live in your words. Help us just to stay—and not quit! In Jesus' name we ask it. Amen.

CHAPTER · 6

Someone To Help

In an earlier chapter I shared my conviction that we do not have a common understanding of the character of God. Some of us carry around ideas of God that are totally at odds with his self-revelation in Jesus. Many of us have false mental images of God that are destructive to our wholeness and joy. I said that we need to listen to Jesus' words about his Father and see in him the revelation of the Father. These same words could be written about our understanding of the Holy Spirit. When I tell a congregation that I am going to preach from the words of Jesus about the Holy Spirit, they usually respond with three sets of attitudes:

Some of them say, "Oh, yes! Let's hear it!"

Some of them say, "Oh, no! Not that!"

Most of them say, "Oh, well. . . ."

Could it be that our neutral or negative feelings about the Holy Spirit persist because we have not listened carefully to what Jesus said about him? Could it be that, here and there, we have picked up concepts about the Spirit without ever having brought them to Jesus?

Let's bring them to Jesus right now. Though we usually turn to the Book of Acts and the writings of Paul for information about the Holy Spirit, Jesus spoke about the Spirit and his ministry, and we must not miss what he had to say. I believe Jesus is a reasonable authority in these matters. He makes four distinct statements in the Farewell Discourse about the Holy Spirit. Let's look at them:

"If you love me, you will keep my commandments. And I will pray the Father, and he will give you another Counselor, to be with you for ever, even the Spirit of truth, whom the world cannot receive, because it neither sees him nor knows him; you know him, for he dwells with you" (John 14:15–17).

"But the Counselor, the Holy Spirit, whom the Father will send in my name, he will teach you all things, and bring to your remembrance all that I have said to you" (v. 26).

"But when the Counselor comes, whom I shall send to you from the Father, even the Spirit of truth, who proceeds from the Father, he will bear witness to me" (15:26).

"Nevertheless I tell you the truth: it is to your advantage that I go away, for if I do not go away, the Counselor will not come to you; but if I go, I will send him to you. . . . When the Spirit of truth comes, he will guide you into all the truth. . . . He will glorify me, for he will take what is mine and declare it to you" (16:7–15).

Let us begin our study by looking at the terms Jesus uses when speaking of Jesus. What does Jesus call him? In each of the sayings, Jesus calls the Holy Spirit our *Paracletos*. This Greek word is variously translated *Counselor* (as in "counselor" at law), *Comforter* (from the Latin *conforiare*, "to strengthen much"), *Advocate,* and *Helper*. Obviously, the Greek word that Jesus used is difficult to translate with one English word. But its basic meaning is "one who is called upon to help another, to intercede on behalf of another." Though it may be hard to find the best English translation of *Paracletos,* it is not hard to understand what Jesus meant.

Jesus is saying that the Holy Spirit is on our side, by our side! He is not "out there" in the ether of outer space somewhere; he is here, where we are, working for us. He is on the same side we are.

A relationship somewhat like that is established in a marriage. Two people come out from the rest of society to stand side by side, on the same side, and they promise to remain on the same side. Sometimes when Mary Jo and I are "discussing" (which is a much better term than *fussing*), one of us will say to the other, "Whose side are you on, anyhow?" Marital partners are prone to forget they are on the same side.

But there is no question about whose side the Holy Spirit is on. Can you really hear that? Can you believe it?

The only other term Jesus uses for the Holy Spirit, besides *Paracletos,* is the phrase "Spirit of truth." We have no translation problem here! Jesus' statements remind me of the familiar words in 1 John: "God is light, and in him is no darkness at all" (1:5). In God there is no caprice, no deceit, no trickery—and his Spirit is the Spirit of truth. His Spirit will not lead us into falsehood; he is not the Spirit of mindless emotion or ecstatic abandon. He is the Spirit of truth by our side, on our side.

What does Jesus say about the ministry of the Holy Spirit? As I reflect on these sayings of Jesus, I conclude that the Spirit's ministry is one of *presence.* The Holy Spirit is God's personal presence with us, here and now. He is the God who revealed himself in Jesus, actively and personally present now. A good short, nontheological definition of the Holy Spirit would be: God in action. Wherever God goes, the Holy Spirit goes; whatever God does, the Holy Spirit does. The Holy Spirit is God's presence in the affairs of the world today.

We easily separate the Holy Spirit from God. Or we consider the Spirit to be divine, yet isolate him from the Godhead. In fact, we have tended to be tritheists instead of trinitarians. What I mean is, at the practical level we believe in three Gods, side by side, instead of one God whose nature is to be a fellowship of three Persons. We evangelical

Christians don't suppose we have three Gods; yet we think and act as if we do.

Our thinking runs something like this: There is God the Father who created us, gave us the Ten Commandments, and will pronounce judgment on us at the Last Day. There is Jesus the Son who loves us, gave us the Sermon on the Mount, and died so that we might be saved from our sins. Then there is the Holy Spirit who fill us or baptizes us or "zaps" us or. . .does whatever it is he does to us!

When we think of God in this way, we develop a concept of three Gods who seems scarcely related to one another. (We may even have a problem knowing to which one we should pray without hurting the others' feelings!) Unfortunately, when we think this way we also develop three Bibles and three kinds of religious experience.

The Father God's Bible is the Old Testament, and his kind of religious experience is condemnation. The Jesus God's Bible is the Gospels of the New Testament, and his type of religious experience is forgiveness and the new birth. The Spirit God's Bible is the Book of Acts and the Epistles, and his sort of religious experience is sanctification or the Spirit-filled life or Spirit baptism. We have begun to think of three Gods, side by side!

But Christians don't believe in three Gods. We believe in one God. We aren't tritheists; we are trinitarians. This means that in the unity of God there is the manifestation of a "threeness" which does not involve three separate entities, but a oneness expressed in holy fellowship. When we speak of God the Father, we are not speaking of someone separate from God; we are merely thinking of God in a certain way. When we speak of God the Son, we are thinking of God in his self-revelation in the incarnate Lord Jesus. And when we speak of the Holy Spirit, we are thinking of God revealed in Jesus *now present* among us, in love and in power. These are three manifestations or personal expressions of the one sovereign God. We know him as Father, Son, and Holy Spirit.

This is not supposed to be a formal lesson on the doctrine of the Trinity. You might say it is just a call to get our Gods together.

I believe the most beautiful privilege I have as a Christian is the opportunity for personal fellowship with God. That fellowship is ours through the ministry of God's own Spirit. Jesus indicated to his disciples that the Holy Spirit would be to them all that his own personal presence had been—and more! We have the privilege of that fellowship, too, through the Spirit's ministry of presence.

Jesus also said that the Holy Spirit would have a ministry of *guidance.* "he will teach you all things, and bring to your remembrance all that I have said to you" (14:26). As we respond to the Holy Spirit, he becomes our teacher. We certainly need one, don't we? I thank God that we don't have to attain a certain level of brilliance to be a Christian; that lets me in!

On the other hand, it is no special blessing to be stupid. When you think about it, we modern Christians are about as stupid as we can be and still get by! We have no time to reflect or meditate on the truly important decisions of life. We have time only to run about, keeping ourselves busy and filling our lives with noise. We don't even have time to know what we believe. When we encounter problems that we can't handle, we fuss and stew and take an aspirin; or we lie down and take a nap, hoping it will pass. When we stumble across strange doctrines with a hundred Bible verses quoted out of context, we get worried and run to our pastor, crying, "What do we believe?"

God can forgive sin, but what can he do with stupidity?

If we will let him, God will be our teacher. If we will listen, he will send his own Spirit to be our guide and teach us his wonderful words.

I have said that Christians like you and me do not take the

words of Jesus as seriously as we should. We are just not sure how they fit into our life in the Spirit. Why is that? Perhaps it goes back to the way we think of God—or rather, our three Gods. You see, if we try to worship an Old Testament Father God who condemns us and a Gospels Jesus who loves and saves us, alongside an Acts and Epistles Holy Spirit who fills and empowers us, where do the words of Jesus apply?

Perhaps our problem has something to do with the way our Bible is put together, at least with the way we read it. We pass from condemnation in the Old Testament to grace and salvation in the Gospels to fullness of the Spirit in Acts and the Epistles. We know that the "native land" of life in the Spirit is Acts and the Epistles, so we prefer to spend much of our study time there. But the question remains: Where do the words of Jesus fit in?

We are experiencing a tremendous groundswell of concern about Christian life and the Spirit, about gifts of the Spirit, about Spirit-activated ministries within the church. So we are reading Acts and 1 Corinthians and Ephesians, dimly aware that the words of Jesus are "back there" somewhere, unheard and unremembered. Let me illustrate: A friend of mine was preaching a series of sermons from the Sermon on the Mount. After a few weeks, one of the dear brothers of the church came to talk with him. He was greatly distressed because the pastor was not preaching "holiness." When my friend told me about this, I thought, *How awful! How can you preach the words of Jesus and NOT preach holiness?* But I understand that concerned brother's feelings, even though I don't agree with them. He wanted his pastor to preach the New Testament call to a holy life. He simply had categories that did not include the words of Jesus:

A sermon on Pentecost. . . *Yes.*

1 Thessalonians 5:23. . . *Yes.*

Hebrews 9:13–14. . . *Amen!*

1 Corinthians 13... *Great!*
The Sermon on the Mount... *What?!*
"What does the Sermon on the Mount have to do with holiness? That sermon was preached before the Holy Spirit came at Pentecost!"

I think this dear brother is not the only one with this problem. Just how do we connect the words of Jesus with the ministry of the Holy Spirit in our lives? Jesus himself gave us the answer if we will hear it. It is the ministry of the Holy Spirit to bring to our remembrance—that is, to help us observe—the words that Jesus spoke. Jesus' words are not back there in the past, made obsolete by the coming of the Spirit. His words are out in front of us. In fact, the words of Jesus are preserved in the Gospels precisely because the early church, filled with the Spirit, remembered them and talked about the things he had done. In the years between the Resurrection and the writing of the Gospels—thirty to sixty years—those Spirit-filled Christians were sharing the parables, rehearsing the miracles, and remembering the narratives of Jesus' life. They were memorizing them, teaching them, preaching them, using them on their evangelistic circuits, and resolving their church problems with them. So when the Evangelists were ready to write, they found the matériel all around them in the memory and life of the church.

I know we can't reverse history, but I wish we could make one change in the sequence of our Bibles: I wish we could take the four Gospels out of the front of the New Testament and place them somewhere around the Epistle to the Hebrews. Chronologically that is about where they belong; and it would remind us that the Holy Spirit kept the words of Jesus fresh in the memory of the church for decades before they were set down on paper.

The Holy Spirit continues his guiding ministry today, and the words of Jesus are his instruments of guidance. When I read the words of Jesus, the Spirit makes me realize they are for me, now!

When Jesus says, "Blessed are the poor in spirit," the Holy Spirit says to me, "Down, boy!" I need to hear that.

When Jesus says, "Judge not," the Holy Spirit says, "Back off." I need to hear that.

When Jesus says, "Forgive your brother," the Holy Spirit reminds me that I need that, too.

Thus the words of Jesus become the data used by the Spirit at the growing edge of my life in Christ.

I am not trying to compare the words of Jesus with the words of Paul, or to say that the Gospel of John is better than the Epistle to James. What I am saying—saying because I am hearing it from Jesus—is that his words are still for me, here and now. They are for all of us who seek to live in his Spirit. In all that Jesus said about the ministry of the Holy Spirit, we find only one word about receiving Christ and remaining in his eternal fellowship: "If you love me, you will keep my commandments. And I will pray the Father, and he will give you another Counselor, to be with you for ever" (John 14:15–16). So the Spirit's daily guidance is vital to my remaining in fellowship with Christ.

Note one final word that Jesus gives us concerning the ministry of the Holy Spirit: "He will glorify me" (16:14). The Holy Spirit has a ministry of exaltation; he lifts up the lifted-up Jesus and exalts the exalted Christ. His ministry is to glorify Jesus. By his personal presence and by his guidance, he places Jesus at the center of our lives.

As Jesus gave substance to our concept of the Father, he also gives substance to our idea of the Holy Spirit. What is God like? He is like Jesus. And what is the Holy Spirit like? He is like Jesus!

· · ● · ·

O Jesus, we thank you for your Holy Spirit, the Spirit of truth, who stands by our side and on our side. We thank you that your presence is made real to us through him.

We open our hearts to your Spirit, Lord. Is there some new word we need to hear from you? Don't let us close our minds and hearts to your Spirit because of false ideas or false mental images of you.

O Spirit of the living Christ, teach us, guide us, and bring home to our hearts the words of our Lord, giving us the grace to obey him. Amen.

CHAPTER · 7

I Am
Who I Am

When Jesus was on earth, he came to us from God, he did the works of God, and he spoke to us on behalf of God. Jesus also came from *us*. he did what we do, talk as we talk, and spoke to God on our behalf! I think the most glorious example of this is found in the seventeenth chapter of John. This passage is called the high priestly prayer because in it the one who comes from God prepares to go back to God. The one who spoke the Father's words to us prays to the Father about us. The one who brought God to where we are *brings us to where God is!* So Jesus fulfills the unique role of a priest in this prayer. He brings God to us and brings us to God.

This is a formal, stylized, incredibly beautiful prayer that seems to gather up all the major themes of Jesus' life and ministry as recorded in John's Gospel. Perhaps we should consider the setting in which it was uttered:

Remember that it is late Thursday evening before Jesus' death on Good Friday. He is with the eleven men who represent the infant church. The words he speaks this night reveal his understanding of himself, his understanding of his followers, and his everlasting concern for his church. They are the words of the incarnate Lord to his infant church on the eve of his sacrificial death for them. They are the words of the risen Lord to his growing church at the time they are written by the old apostle. They are the words of our interceding priest to his abiding church today, tomorrow, and forever. So let us read these words reverently:

I have manifested thy name to the men whom thou gavest me out of the world; thine they were, and thou gavest them to me, and they have kept thy word. Now they know that everything that thou hast given me is from thee; for I have given them the words which thou gavest me, and they have received them and know in truth that I came from thee; and they have believed that thou didst send me. I am praying for them; I am not praying for the world but for those whom thou hast given me, for they are thine; all mine are thine, and thine are mine, and I am glorified in them. And now I am no more in the world, but they are in the world, and I am coming to thee. Holy Father, keep them in thy name, which thou hast given me; I have guarded them, and none of them is lost but the son of perdition, that the scripture might be fulfilled. But now I am coming to thee; and these things I speak in the world, that they may have my joy fulfilled in themselves. I have given them thy word; and the world has hated them because they are not of the world, even as I am not of the world. I do not pray that thou shouldst take them out of the world, but that thou shouldst keep them from the evil one. They are not of the world, even as I am not of the world. Sanctify them in the truth; thy word is truth. As thou didst send me into the world, so I have sent them into the world. And for their sake I consecrate myself, that they also may be consecrated in truth.

I do not pray for these only, but also for those who believe in me through their word, that they may all be one; even as thou, Father, art in me, and I in thee, that they also may be in us, so that the world may believe that thou hast sent me. The glory which thou hast given me I have given to them, that they may be one even as we are one, I in them and thou in me, that they may become perfectly one, so that the world may know that thou hast sent me and hast loved them even as thou hast loved me. Father, I desire that they also, whom thou hast given me, may be with me where I am, to behold my glory which thou hast given me in thy love for me before the foundation of the world. O righteous Father, the world has not known thee, but I have known thee; and these know that thou hast sent me. I made known to them thy name, and I will make it known, that the love with which thou hast loved me may be in them, and I in them (John 17:6–26).

In this magnificent prayer, Jesus shares with his Father the things he has accomplished during his earthly stay. "I have manifested thy name to the men whom thou hast given me out of the world. I have made known to them thy name, and I will make it known" (vv. 6, 26).

Jesus gives us God's name. Names today don't have a great deal of what we might call prophetic significance. That is, our names do not say anything special about our character or convictions. I know a girl named Faith, but she is not any more trusting than a Karen or a Debbie. When our first daughter was born, we named her Pamela Ann. As I think about it now, I'm not sure why; it just seemed like a good name at the time. My name is Reuben; along with me, others have at times wondered why! (When I was born, in the front bedroom of a farmhouse, my grandfather was back East preaching. Though everyone called him "Uncle Buddy," his real name was Reuben. I have been told that when he heard I had been born, he sent my mother a money order for fifty dollars—so she named me Reuben! I haven't had any problems with my name from that time till this, because I understand perfectly why I am named Reuben. And if you had sent me a check for fifty dollars when my first daughter was born, I would have named her after you!)

But a biblical name was not just a label of identification; it expressed the essential character of the person who bore the name. A person's name was supposed to reveal his character. This is why Esau said of his deceiving brother, "Is he not rightly named Jacob? For he has supplanted me these two times" (Gen. 27:36). The name *Jacob* in the Old Testament meant "one who takes by the heel." After twenty years of deception and fraud, Jacob met God at Peniel. In the soul-wrenching struggle of a wrestling match, the messenger of God said to him, "What is your name?" And he replied, "Jacob." Then he said, "Your name shall no longer be called Jacob, but Israel" (Gen. 32:28). *Israel* literally meant "one who prevails with God." The name reflected the character; and when the character changed, the name changed!

Aren't you glad that we are not obliged to fulfill the meaning of our names? When real changes take place, we are not bound to old names and old ways. In fact, God has promised each one of us a new name: "You shall be called by a new name which the mouth of the Lord will give" (Isa. 62:2).

What about God's name? Surely God's name also stands for his character. To know the name of God is to know him. His name reveals something of the way he wants to be known. As with other biblical names, the name and person of God go together. This is why the Bible says, "You shall not take the name of the Lord your God in vain" (Exod. 20:7). "To take the name in vain" is to dishonor the person of God. It also explains why Jesus taught us to pray, "Our Father who art in heaven, hallowed be thy name" (Matt. 6:9). To "hallow the name" of the Father is to reverence him.

When we speak the name of God, we are not expressing a magic, power-filled word that changes things when it is spoken. But the name reminds us of God's very nature; it refreshes our understanding of the one with whom we live in intimate daily relationship. God revealed himself to the nation of Israel by the Hebrew name *Yahweh,* which may be translated,

I am who I am.
I am because I am.
I will be what I will be.
I cause to be whatever exists.

What does that mean? It is difficult to know exactly. Perhaps the difficulty is intentional, for the mystery of God cannot be fully captured in one term, but in the way he makes himself known through his actions. He is indeed what he is; truly he accomplishes whatever he says.

From the time of Moses, the Israelites knew God by his Yahweh name as the great "I Am." As time passed, the sacredness of his name was emphasized more and more until the Jews feared to pronounce it, even in worship. Then Jesus came! Jesus, the incarnate "I Am," broke the silence of history and spoke the name of God once again through his own giving, loving, surrendered life. Jesus came not only *knowing* the name of God but *bearing* the name of God. He became the ultimate revelation of God to his people. In Old Testament times, God instructed his people to worship at the place where he put his name—at the tabernacle and later the temple. Jesus' own person replaced the tabernacle/temple. He fulfilled the promise of God's presence; he became the place where we meet God. He is the place where God has put his name.

Have you ever wandered out under the stars in a time of deep longing and loneliness, feeling the pain of human weakness, and cried, "God, who are you?"

The answer to that question cannot be given in a simple term or a label. And if a deep, holy voice would answer your cry of existential anguish, saying, "I am Yahweh!" I think you would say through your tears, "Please, God, that's not what I had in mind."

At some time or other, each one of us does cry out, "God, who are you? What is your name?" And that heart-cry is answered in the life of Jesus. He has given us God's name; he has shown us the Father.

God knows me and calls me by name. He knows you by your very own special name. And he has told us his name. So we know each other better than we might think!

· · ● · ·

O God, sometimes we say like Philip, "Show us the Father." And sometimes we cry out, "Who are you, God?" You know the inner hunger that prompts that cry.

In the midst of the mystery of our lives, we need more than your name. We want to know who you are. We want to know where you are. And then we want to know you with the personal intimacy that permits us to call you by name!

We thank you for revealing yourself to us through our Lord Jesus Christ. Because you are the Christlike God, we are sure that you know our names. We are your people who know your name—the essence of the real you. And we thank you for coming to us in Jesus. Amen.

CHAPTER · 8

Give Me
Your Glories

Part of the wonder of the priestly prayer of John 17 is that we are privileged to overhear Jesus as he talks with his Father about himself. In the last chapter we heard him say, "I have manifested thy name..." (v. 6). Now let's listen to another word our Lord speaks about himself; it is the beautiful word, *glory:*

> All mine are thine, and thine are mine, and I am glorified in them. . . . The glory which thou hast given me I have given them, that they may be one even as we are one. . . . Father, I desire that they also, whom thou hast given me, may be with me where I am, to behold my glory which thou hast given me in thy love for me before the foundation of the world (vv. 10, 22, 24).

Jesus gives us God's name and shows us God's glory. I have been thinking about the implications of the word *glory.* This word is used in the Bible to refer to those encounters of the divine and the human, in which the presence of God meets the earthly scene. *Glory* describes a situation in which God's presence is somehow made known to man. When God appears in a bush that burns but is not consumed, there is glory. When God encounters Moses, his man on the mountain, there is glory. When God meets his people anywhere, under any circumstances, there is glory.

In the Old Testament, the word *glory* carries with it the idea of "weight" or "substance." Even in the New Testament, Paul speaks of an "eternal weight of glory" (2 Cor. 4:17). The word connotes something that a person possesses, causing others to give him reverence or respect. In biblical times, the people who were "portly" (Isn't that a kind way to say it?) were those who had enough money to buy the food to become portly! So you might say that a portly person carried a lot of weight in the community— physically and otherwise! Knowing this, it isn't hard to see how the meaning of the word could move from "weight" to influence, respect, and value. A person's glory (literally, his "weight") is that which gives his or her life influence, value, and meaning.

The biblical term *glory* also seems to carry with it the idea of shining, so that a good synonym for glory would be *radiance*. Radiance is an observable phenomenon. The traditional wedding write-ups in a local newspaper usually describe the brides as *radiant*. That term is never used of the groom. I don't know how to define radiance, but we recognize it when we see it, don't we? I am getting bolder about asking young married couples how they are getting along: "How are you doing? How is married life? Do you still love her/him? Are you still speaking?" But I find that I don't really need to ask those questions to gather the information; I can tell by looking at people how they are getting along with their mates. What gives their lives that radiance, joy, lift, and light? Their reflection of *glory* is enough to make me want some!

Jesus said, "The glory which thou hast given me I have given to them, that they may be one even as we are one."

I have been around a college campus long enough to observe that every September a new crop of freshmen arrive, bearing their glories with them. All the local "teen talent" winners are going to take the campus by storm. So at the first parties and social mixers, these people gather around the piano and shove each other off the bench to do their thing. They are the singers and the players and the guitar pickers. Of course the high school superjocks are among them. So are the eggheads! It's funny to see how we tend to show off our "glories" at times. When I see it, I don't know whether to laugh or cry. Because during those first few days on campus, there is a kind of shuffling of glories; and those who do a lot of laughing at the parties sometimes go back to their rooms to cry because their glories have been shuffled aside and their identities have been threatened.

Look at your local church through this perspective for a moment. There are some people in your congregation whose glory lies in their ability to play the piano or the organ; if you don't believe it, try to get them off the bench! There are some ladies in your church whose glory is in their cooking expertise, and they can hardly wait for the next potluck supper; they are the ones who bring the dishes that everybody *has* to have some of! That is their glory. Some fellows know all the names of all the football players on all the major-league teams. That's their thing. Other people glory in their wardrobe; they shop for the right labels at the right places. I know some preachers whose glory is in their books; the books serve roughly the same purpose as wallpaper, only thicker and more impressive.

What's your glory?

For a long time I have pondered the meaning of this message from Jesus: "The glory which thou hast given me I have given them, that they may be one even as we are one." As I think about this verse, I have begun to discover a strange dichotomy in our lives. On the one hand, our glory is that which gives us meaning and weight and substance and clout. On the other hand, those very things divide and fragment us. Do you know why? Because we find our glory on our own "turf." Don't ask me to define that term; all I know is that when I'm on my "turf" and the opposition gets a little close, I become defensive. I suspect this is not the kind of glory that Jesus prayed I would receive.

Here is another awesome word of Jesus in John 5:55: "How can you believe, who receive glory from one another and do not seek the glory that comes from the only God?" Think about that. It's a fascinating set of dynamics. If I'm a red-hot ukelele player and nobody knows about it, how will I get my clout? On the other hand, if I perform and then you prove to be a better ukelele player, I feel threatened and this separates us. This is the kind of glory we receive from one another. But Jesus was praying about "The glory which thou [Father] hast given me. . . ."

What was Jesus' glory? What gave him his meaning and value, his authority and confidence, his radiance throughout life? It certainly wasn't where he lived, for he said, "Foxes have holes, and the birds of the air have nests; but the Son of man has nowhere to lay his head" (Matt. 8:20). I don't think his glory was in what he wore, though he did have a seamless robe (John 19:23). He had some good people around him, but I doubt that his authority lay in his ability to choose and direct personnel. One of his followers betrayed him, one of them denied him, and the whole bunch fled under pressure; individually, they weren't very special people. Jesus was a great preacher-teacher and I am sure he had a sense of joy and fulfillment in sharing the truth with others. Yet during the most popular phase of his ministry, he had an underlying mood of disappointment because the people did not see what he wanted them to see or hear what he wanted them to hear. So wherein was Jesus' glory?

I have come to believe that it was in his total dependence upon his Father. Throughout his life Jesus said, ". . .I have come down from heaven, not to do my own will, but the will of him who sent me" (John 6:38). ". . .The words that I say to you I do not speak on my own authority; but the Father who dwells in me does his works" (John 10:14). ". . .I seek not my own will but the will of him who sent me" (John

5:30). Jesus' glory was in the totality of his dependence upon his Father, in his obedience to his Father, and in his profound awareness that his Father was in control of all the affairs of life.

If my glory rests in something that I can do, I will be greatly disturbed when I meet someone who can do it better. If my glory depends on the people I know, then I am vulnerable to depression when those people let me down. So I live defensively, under tension and fear. But if I yield my glories to God, so that I derive my sense of worth and value from my relationship with my heavenly Father, then when I meet someone who has more books than I have, or has read more of them, or can preach better than I can, it doesn't hurt quite as much! In fact, that relationship with the Father makes it possible for us to maintain the unity of the Spirit in the bond of peace amidst the diversity of gifts we have within the body of Christ.

· · ● · ·

Isn't it strange that the very gifts that were intended to help us Christians be what we are, do what we do, and develop unity in the body seem to divide us? Perhaps this has come about because of a subtle shift in attitude from total dependence upon God to dependence upon the gift, so that a person's own worth is supposed to be found in what God has done for the individual, not in God himself.

Jesus found his glory in the depth of his surrender to his heavenly Father. When the crowds flattered him, he did not lose his poise; when they rejected him, he did not lose his nerve; when they crucified him, he did not lose his love. Imagine the tragic wreck he might have made of his life if he gloried in his supernatural gifts.

Of course, we always have a fundamental need for self-worth and meaning; and to a large measure we find that self-worth in what we are able to do. I hope you know that you can do something well. It is terrible to grow up feeling, "I can't do anything right," or "I'm a nobody." Every person needs a sense of self-worth, self-confidence, and self-acceptance. But when those things become the ground of our glory, we put ourselves up for grabs. We begin to depend upon the recognition and praise of people around us to maintain our self-based image.

Yet if we take our gifts and talents to the cross, we can use them without being personally destroyed and without dividing the body of Christ. I am hearing the familiar words of the apostle Paul: ". . .Far be it from me to glory except in the cross of our Lord Jesus Christ. . ." (Gal. 6:14).

· · ● · ·

Father, what is my glory? Don't let me back away from that probing question. Do I find my meaning and self-worth in something other than you? If so, I give my little glories to you. Let your glory become my glory.

Father, I know that some people reading these words are saying, "I don't have any glory. I can't do anything. I don't have any worthwhile gift. I don't even know what radiance means!" Please let them find their worth in you. Let them find their meaning in your love, their purpose in your will, and their radiance in your fellowship. I ask it in your name—and for your glory. Amen.

CHAPTER · 9

Hunger
To Be Holy

In the priestly prayer the thoughts of Jesus go far beyond himself. We hear him share with his Father his concerns for those of us who are his disciples. Jesus prayed for us on that awesome night. Read again these words: "I am not praying for the world but for those whom thou hast given me, for *they are thine*" (17:9, italics mine).

May I ask you a very personal question? *To whom do you belong?* Let me put it another way: To whom are you fully present?

Perhaps you recall times when you felt in the midst of conversation that you were really "missing." Your mind and heart were somewhere else. We have some students at our college who registered in September but who have never been present. Their bodies are here; they report to class; a certain amount of work occurs at the ends of their pencils. But they are absent!

Where are you totally present?

We know instinctively that we belong to God and that we need to be in his presence. Disciples belong to God; that really settles the matter of ownership, doesn't it? But are we fully present in fellowship with him, or are we "missing persons"?

Jesus said another thing in this passage that fascinates me.

He said, "They are in the world." Reread the full context of that statement: "And now I am no more in the world, but *they are in the world,* and I am coming to thee. . . . I do not pray that thou shouldst take them out of the world, but that thou shouldst keep them from the evil one" (vv. 11, 15, italics mine).

That statement helps me understand where my Christian discipleship is really supposed to be. Many of us assume that our discipleship should be lived in an unreal world; we suppose that if we were as disciplined or as committed as we ought to be, our lives would be "out of this world." But Jesus has an insight for us at this point. He didn't pray that we live outside the real world, but in it. Remember the old gospel song:

> This world is not my home,
> I'm just a-passing through,
> My treasures are laid up
> Somewhere beyond the blue.
> —Albert Brumley

That's not a bad lyric—except for the fact that it isn't true! Many of the songs we sing and sermons we've heard have communicated essentially this same idea: We don't belong in this world. But Jesus says we do! True, we are just passing through this mortal world; but it is still our home. We belong here.

Many of us have developed the "if only" syndrome. We feel that "if things were only different," we could serve Christ more faithfully. Often I have thought, *If only my house were arranged differently, I could be a better Christian. . . .* My house has a den connected to the living room, with a sliding glass door between. The living room is where we have good light and comfortable chairs where I can sit and read the Bible and meditate and. . .be holy. But the trouble is, just a few feet away in the den is the television set. It's hard for me to be holy in the living room when, out of the corner of my eye, I can see the television and hear things that sound so interesting. I don't like television, of course; but on occasion I look up just in time to see some dastardly deed done to a fellow primate. And I say, "Well, how come that?" So an hour and forty-seven commercials later, I'm not as holy as I was before! So you see, my house is just not set up for me to be holy in. I guess I could go to the kitchen to be holy; but the refrigerator is there. Or I could go and be holy in the bedroom; but the bed is there. I need to add another room onto our house for me to be holy in—but Mary Jo would put the sewing machine in there!

I could be more holy if I didn't have to drive the freeway to work. I'm not kidding! Day after day, I set out from home to go and be a blessing to my students at school; and by the time I get there, I'm the one who needs prayer. I leave home at a quarter of seven in the morning and the freeway is already full of dumbhead people who crowd the lanes and give stupid signals! You understand what I'm saying, don't you?

I could be a better Christian if only people would quit bothering me at work. During the years that I was campus chaplain, I wanted to tack up a sign:

I'm your friendly, loving chaplain.
Tuesdays and Thursdays, 2:00 to 4:00.

or,

Do Not Disturb.
Being Holy!

I once wrote a book entitled *We Really Do Need Each Other.* Now I'm working on a sequel: *Will Everybody Please Leave Me Alone?*

I am sure you could be more holy if only you had a

different roommate, if you had a better car (or even a car), if you had a different job, if your spouse were different, if you house were different . . . if . . . if . . . if. . . .

For too long, the basic presuppositions of my life have been these kinds of things, every one of which is fundamental to my living in this world. Home, family, TV, work, people, the car—these are the things of my common, daily life! I have begun to see that the "if only" syndrome leads to isolation and exclusiveness, a rejection of the created world, a turning away from God's order. This kind of thinking imposes a kind of superspirituality upon the naturalness of life, denying the validity of my existence. Yet this world is still my home.

We are not going to live here forever. But in the meantime, *did you know that we live here?* We have sounds to hear and ears to hear them. We have places to go and feet to walk there. We have people to love and arms to hug them. We have people who need our caring and hearts to care. We have words to say and lips to speak them. Why, if we didn't know any better, we might think we were made to be here.

Jesus said, "They are in the world. I do not pray that thou shouldst take them out of the world but that thou shouldst keep them from the evil one" (17:11, 15). I believe that God's will for us is not so much to be separated from the things of the world as to be separated from our own false selves—set free to live in his world and use his "things" for his glory.

My responsibilities take me out of town from time to time. And I have reasonable assurance, based on the law of averages, that something will go wrong at home while I am away. Some part of my car will need to be repaired. My office will be piled higher with mail and stuff that needs to be done. But whatever goes wrong, this is still my world. And I hear Jesus saying that he has given me everything he has promised in this world where I live. Granted, the life I live in the Lord is indeed a life of tension; the tension is found in the two statements: "They are thine." And, "They are in the world." Christian disciples belong to God, but they are in the world. We have not fully realized the ambivalent character of living "between the times." We live between the time of birth and death, the first and second coming, the time of our entering into life in Christ and being made perfect with him in glory. Yet amidst the tensions that are part of our human existence, we belong to God and our participation is in the world. We ought to recognize that it is not a simple thing to be an obedient disciple in the world.

I wonder if we haven't developed a kind of religion that makes us think we are supposed to be more spiritual than Jesus? Our religion has a tendency to move toward spirituality and away from the world. Yet somehow Jesus was able to keep both right where they belong. How? And what does he want us to do, being in the world yet not of it? Let me gather some verses from this seventeenth chapter that point us toward an answer: "Sanctify them in the truth; thy word is truth. As thou didst send me into the world, so I have sent them into the world. And for their sake I consecrate myself, that they may also be consecrated in truth" (vv. 17–19). Jesus' prayer for his in-the-world church is that it be holy; his heart's desire for us real-world people is that we be holy. If we want to understand what he expects of us, we must grapple with the meaning of the word *holy*.

· · ● · ·

In the Greek language all the words relating to the idea of *holy* sound alike because they all come from one basic word, *hagios*. In our English language our holiness vocabulary comes from two word families. The Anglo-Saxons gave us the words *holy* and *holiness,* while the Latins gave us *sanctity, sanctify,* and *sanctification.* Both word families convey the same meaning; I wish they all had the same sound.

For many people the sounds of these great words have grown old and dull. For others they have become symbols of exclusive doctrines or standards of spiritual achievement and status. Thus these words have lost their luster and allure for many Christians.

I suppose it is too late to change the way our holiness words sound. But it is not too late to discover again the glory and power of what they mean. I perceive in God's people a growing heart-hunger to be holy. In fact, this hunger may be at the core of all other human hungers. This hunger to be holy is the God-shaped vacuum in the heart of every person. Oddly enough, though the hunger persists, it is seldom expressed. I don't know whether we can find new terms that would help us express this hunger; but I do know that each one of us has a hunger to be holy. Our hunger reflects the Lord's profound heart-hunger that his church be sanctified, holy, and "meet for the Master's use" (2 Tim. 2:21 KJV).

· · ● · ·

What does Jesus mean when he prays for us to be made holy? At the end of the Bible studies and the journal articles and the textbook examinations, it seems to me that one great idea emerges: *To be holy means to be different by virtue of belonging to God.* The first important word to notice in that sentence is *belonging.* Only God is holy in any original sense—in his separateness, his purity, his wholeness—and other things or persons become holy by virtue of their relationship with God. That is why the Israelite temple, along with its vestments and ceremonial utensils, could be considered holy; all of those things belonged uniquely to

God. Then what must we say of holy *people?* Fundamentally, the Bible says that people likewise are holy because they belong to God. So when Jesus prays that we become holy, he is asking that our wills and intentions be entirely devoted to God and to his service. All of our talents, all of our energies, indeed our lives in their entirety, should be marked with the seal of consecration. The seal of consecration implies a renouncing of self, just as Jesus was willing to renounce all of his heavenly claims in order to serve his Father on earth. That is a radical belonging to God.

We find another example of the seal of consecration when we consider the history of Israel in the Old Testament. Israel was nothing apart from the initiative of God. Into the flow of human history came the tiny nation of Israel, called into being by God. We do not know a great deal about the background of other ancient nations; but we do know about Abraham, Isaac, and Jacob, the patriarchs of Israel. We know that God brought these people out of Egypt and made them his people at the foot of Sinai. We know that God entered into a covenant relationship with them. And God said, "I don't call you because you are beautiful, wise, good, or powerful. I have simply chosen to set my love upon you. I have called you." Apart from that calling, Israel was nothing.

Why did Israel's prophets keep warning them, "Don't get involved with Assyria. . . . Don't get involved with Babylon. . . . Don't get involved with Egypt. . . . Put your trust in God·. . . "? It wasn't because the prophets were political neutralists, but because they saw that Israel existed by virtue of one reason—their relationship with God. When Israel moved away from that fundamental dependency, they proved false to their true identity, and trouble followed.

We can bring this lesson into the New Testament and apply it to the people of the new covenant, the new Israel—the church of God. From where does the church come? We did't create it; God did. The church is his idea. He brought it into being in the new Exodus consummated on the cross.

Liberated by the power of his Spirit, we move out under the sign of the cross as the new Israel, the chosen people of God. And God says to us, I didn't call you because you were good or great or anything special. You are what you are simply because you belong to me and have been called into existence by my Word.

Suddenly, we find ourselves in the midst of a New Testament ethic that says, "Be what you are! Be a Christ-person." For Jesus says, "Apart from me, you can do nothing." To be holy then means to put at the center of our lives what is in fact the center of our lives. We are to be Christ-people, fully devoted to serving our heavenly Father. Holiness means God-centeredness, being separated unto him, belonging to the community that is his exclusive possession.

When we realize that God is intrinsically holy, we understand why we need cleansing and a liberation from the power of the carnal mind in the process of moving into a holy relationship with him. If we are to belong to the community that belongs to God, we need the cleansing and empowering of his Holy Spirit. I am hearing the words of an old invitational hymn:

> Break down every idol,
> Cast out every foe.
> —James Nicholson

As the Word of God penetrates my life, I find that it has increasing power and magnetism; it makes expanding demands upon me; and it speaks reassuringly about who I am—a Christ person.

The second important word in our definition of holiness is *different.* We become different by belonging to God. As it was with the old Israel, so with the new Israel. Old Israel was different from the surrounding nations because every part of their life was related to God. The Israelite people were to reflect God's character and will as spelled out in the Book of the Covenant. For us of the new covenant, the same dynamics apply. Our radical belonging to God results in lives that reflect God's character and will.

What does that mean for me personally? It means that I am to live in growing likeness to Jesus through the power of his Spirit. That is my most overt expression of radically belonging to him. Jesus said, Don't take them out of the world, Father. "As thou hast sent me, I have sent them. Sanctify them through thy truth. Thy word is truth. As thou hast sent me, I have sent them. And for their sake, I sanctify myself that they may be sanctified in the truth."

At the very core of the matter, holiness means God-centeredness, Christlikeness, and God-sentness. That is the prayer of Jesus for us. We are in the world, sent to the world. And if we are going to be persons who put God at the center of our lives and proclaim God to the world, we must do it with the rooms of our homes arranged as they are. We may have to learn to like our cars the way they are. We may need to accept the intrusion of people around us to whom we want to shout, "Would you please leave me alone so I can be holy?" The word of the Lord comes to us in the world in which we live and to which we are sent. To that word we say, "Yes, Lord!"

· · ● · ·

O God, the holy God, here we are in our world. The house, the job, the room, the people, the things, the responsibilities. . . (Would you stop praying now and visualize *your* world with your home, your family, your relationships?) *O Father, we say yes to our world. Don't let us think we can become more holy by leaving it, in fact or in fancy. We know it is not your will to take us out of it.*

Help us enter into our world by your Spirit in a deeper way than ever before. We open our world to you. Break down every idol. Cast out every foe. We would be your holy people—God-centered, Christlike, and sent to minister in the world where we live. Amen.

CHAPTER · 10

We Are Together

An objective analysis of the priestly prayer would reveal that it is the prayer of Jesus for the oneness of his church. Again and again, that petition is heard. It is his first clear petition for his disciples: "I am praying for them. . . . Holy Father, keep them in thy name, which thou hast given me, that they may be one, even as we are one" (vv. 9a, 11).

Let me share what the Lord has been laying on my heart concerning these verses. Our priority for oneness in the community of believers is far lower on our scale of values than it is for our Lord. Oneness in the community was an extremely high priority for him and for the writers of the New Testament. If we started listing our priorities, I am sure it would be there somewhere; most Christians would agree that oneness is important. But do we think it is absolutely essential?

Jesus considered oneness to be a vital issue for the infant church. And he included all the rest of us when he said, "I do not pray for these only, but also for those who are to believe in me through their word, that they may all be one . . . that they may become perfectly one, so that the world may know. . ." (vv. 20, 23). I am overwhelmed to think how significant the matter of oneness is in the mind of Jesus, compared to what it means to me. The oneness he intended for us transcends all cultural barriers that normally divide us. Undoubtedly you have sung Samuel J. Stone's great hymn of the church, one verse of which goes like this:

> Yet she on earth hath union
> with God the Three in One,
> And mystic sweet communion
> With those whose rest is won.

This means that the church, the visible body of Christ, is part of all those of all the ages who are part of the blood-washed body of Christ. It means that our oneness encompasses all of time. Think about that for a moment: Think of all the cultures, lifestyles, and languages that Christians have known across the centuries. And Jesus prayed, "Make them one!"

I have a mental image I want to share with you. I would like you to go with me once more to that Upper Room on the evening of the Last Supper. Can you see that room? Can you picture Jesus at the head of the table? Can you imagine the disciples assembled at their places? There they are, the group of twelve, their elbows on the table in fellowship and intimacy. Now I want you to imagine that you are taking out the end wall of that room; just take out the wall and lengthen the table so that it is long enough to seat all the Christians of the first century. Let them come. Now lengthen the table again and invite the Christians of the second century to take their places. Let the table grow longer, longer, and longer until at last it comes to rest where you are right now.

Who is sitting at that table? All the saints of the ages are there. (Adjust the color.) Can you see the robes, the hair, the skin? Can you see all the shades and hues at the table? Can you see the various costumes and lifestyles ? Can you see the guests' positions in history? (Now turn up the audio.) Can you hear what they are saying? Listen to their conversations. Listen to their songs. Listen to the hubbub of their villages and towns.

Look at the table again. We are there, sitting with the saints of all the ages! Why are we there? Because we have been invited by the man at the head of the table *to share his life.* What are we doing here? We're passing the bread—the shared, broken life of Jesus. And we are one!

That's what we have in common with other Christians. Any talk about the oneness of the body must be expressed in terms of the life we share around that table. All of us know that the Lord's Supper is the supreme symbol of the oneness of the body of Christian believers, because at that table we share—not our commonality, our congeniality, nor our common heritage—but the shared life of Jesus. And that is enough to make us one.

I remember when I first became the chaplain of a Christian college. I thought it would be heaven on earth in terms of oneness. Look at all the things the students have in common: the same age group, the same culture, the same religious heritage, the same socioeconomic status, the same ideals and goals. What a place for fellowship! What an atmosphere for oneness in Christ! But I discovered that even in the midst of such Christian community, there can be be loneliness, fragmentation, judgmentalism, separation, status symbols, and cliques. I learned that on the campus of this Christian college, three or four weeks into the term, one girl had never gone to the dining hall. She ate all her meals out of vending machines in the dormitory. She was so lonely and insecure that she was afraid to go to the dining hall! I doubt it would have helped for me to tell her, "Your problem is that you're neurotic." ("Oh, thanks! I'll go to the dining hall now!")

I discovered something else as chaplain: Multiplying activities didn't bring oneness, either. We said that we needed to have more interdorm parties because people were lonely and didn't get together enough. But the more parties we had, the more occasions we provided for lonely people to feel lonely! The more dating events we provided, the more we compounded students' misery at not being dated. I began to realize that all of the superficial things we thought would bring us together—didn't!

Only one thing will bring us together; that is our oneness in the Lord. That is why I am excited about the potential for Bible study groups, prayer fellowships, and Christian sharing groups. If such groups are meeting in your community—great! Have some more. If not, why not start one? We need more places to get together around the Word and around our true oneness in the Lord. When we are affirming our oneness in him, we are in fact being what we are called to be. That's when the loneliness breaks down and the openness begins. There is the joy of Christian living.

· · ● · ·

I am chagrined at the petty things that divide us, when in truth the oneness that we have in Christ is the great reality of the Christian life. Not only must the petty things bow, but the important things of our lives must bow before our oneness in Christ.

Several years ago my wife and I spent some time in West Germany, where I spoke to an American military congregation. Now picture this congregation—one family from North Dakota, another family from California, another from Alabama, another from Oklahoma, another from Kansas, and another from Michigan—each bringing its own perception of what a church ought to be. They came to the worship service thinking, *We're in a strange land, but praise the Lord. There are a bunch of good Christians here!* Yet when they came together in the service, they discovered some ideas that seemed very strange. (So did we!) Some wanted old-fashioned revival preaching while others wanted encounter groups. Some wanted to sing, "Holy, Holy, Holy" while others wanted "Do, Lord!" Some wanted a guitar while others wanted an organ. Here all of them were, coming from the same denomination with such different expectations.

To complicate things further, since it was a military congregation, there were a lieutenant colonel and a sergeant on the same church governing board. (My guess is that at the church board meetings the sergeant would say, "I move we vote by secret ballot!")

My visit to that congregation was a time of rich insight. The Lord began to deal with me about Christian oneness and fellowship. I don't know whether Mary Jo and I were much of a blessing to that group, but they were a tremendous blessing to us! In that congregation were all of the factors that could divide and alienate the body of Christ; yet they had beautiful fellowship with one another. At the center of their oneness was a clear awareness of the cross on which their prejudices, expectations, and desires were nailed for the sake of the body. They reminded me of something the apostle Paul said:

> There is neither Jew nor Greek, there is neither slave nor free, there is neither male nor female; for you are all one in Christ Jesus (Gal. 3:28).

As I think about that verse, I realize that the oneness of Christ's body is greater than personal prejudice, rank, sex, or nationality.

Have you ever visited a country where another language was spoken almost exclusively? We got along fairly well in Germany because I knew a few phrases: *Auf wiedersehen, Entschuldigen Sie!* ("Good-bye" and "Pardon me!") But when Mary Jo and I went shopping in downtown Frankfurt and needed some directions, nobody understood or cared. Have you ever been in such a predicament? You get a desperate, isolated feeling. You assume the other people are a bit stupid, so you talk LOUDER! But they still don't understand. Do you suppose we could lay down our nationalistic pride before the oneness of the body of Christ?

Can we lay down our social status, so that we regard no other Christian as "bond or free"? Can we lay down our sexuality so that we no longer regard "male or female"? How much Jesus cares about this! So much that on the night before he died, the dominant theme of his prayer was that we affirm and strengthen the oneness that is ours in the shared life of Christ.

Don't let anyone or anything separate you in your fellowship of believers. What was true of that church in Frankfurt can be true of every body of Christians; there can be mutuality and unity despite great diversity in the fellowship.

What separates you from the Christians around you? Whatever it is, it is not important enough.

Is it denominationalism? Some denominations are conservative; others are liberal. There are plenty of differences between various Christian groups. But the differences are not enough to separate you from other Christians.

Is it your lifestyle ? Are you struggling to keep up with the Joneses, so you feel obliged to attend a higher-class church? Are the Joneses struggling to keep up with you? Nothing matters more than your oneness with them.

Look again at what Jesus prayed: "Make them one *that the world may know. . . .*" If we want to make an impact on our world for Jesus Christ, the things that separate us must bow to his lordship. We are masters at splitting; we know how to defend our personal stand "as a matter of principle" (meaning, to protect our egos). Yet Jesus says we should not let anything separate us; nor should we talk about maintaining our principles in the midst of division. I think of our Lord, ". . .who, though he was in the form of God, did not count equality with God a thing to be grasped, but emptied himself, taking the form of a servant, being born in the likeness of men" (Phil. 2:6–7). Jesus did not lay aside what he had; he laid aside what he was. His example challenges me.

God wills that we be one people. Neither our language nor our culture nor our heritage nor all the things that make us what we are must separate us. We must ultimately bow at the foot of the cross, so that our oneness in Christ may merge. If the Holy Spirit would sweep over individual communities of believers until all the superficial barriers were broken down, and we would affirm each other and live in our oneness in Christ, the blessing and grace of God would be manifested in ways we might never dream. The world would know—and the world would believe in Jesus Christ.

Let us bow down now and place on the altar our nationality, our status, our prejudices, our all. Let's bow before the man at the head of the table—and pass the bread!

· · ● · ·

O Jesus, who prayed that we might be one and who died to make it so, we come to you with all the things that are so important to us and that divide us so much. What must be done to make us one?

We thank you for our church families. I thank you for my own beloved denomination. But let us all know again that we belong to you—that we need each other. Don't allow anything to divide us. Don't allow us to defend our rights at the cost of the integrity of your body. This is difficult for us, Lord. But bring us to the cross and help us see how much it means to you. Give us the grace to affirm it and live it. In your name and by your power we pray. Amen.

C H A P T E R · 11

I Vote Yes
On You!

At the very close of Jesus' high priestly prayer, he makes a very significant statement about love: "I will make known [thy name], that the love with which thou hast loved me may be in them, and I in them" (17:26).

Every Christian knows that God is love. By the same token, love expresses God. Love is our felt oneness behaviorized, actualized in practice, and manifested in discernible acts of Christlike caring. Fundamentally, we Christians *are* one; and if we really believe it, we will behave it. We will not look at one another in a condemning way. We will care for one another as unique persons. We will affirm one another.

Love is. . .

    caring for persons as persons,

    releasing persons,

    steadfastly refusing to judge other persons.

In plain English love means "I vote yes on you!" Love means, on the basis of our oneness in Christ, "I affirm you."

· · ● · ·

Affirm—that's a good word, isn't it? What it really means is, when the vote is in, I am on the affirmative side; I am for you. I vote yes on you as a person. That doesn't mean I like everything you do or approve of the way you act. Not at all. Let me give you some examples of what affirmation is not, since opposites may help us to understand concepts better:

We drive into the church parking lot. Just as we pull in, another car parks nearby. We glance over to see who it is. *Oh, no!* We walk into the sanctuary, sit down, and there is that same person beside us. *Oh, no!* We open the bulletin and read that Sister So-and-So is singing today. *Oh, no!* The pastor's sermon will be on tithing. *Oh, no!*

After we get home, the phone rings and we pick it up. *Oh, no!* The doorbell rings and we open the door. *Oh, no!*

We can develop a "no" vote on those who are closest to us, can't we? I know some husbands who are forever saying no to their wives. Every communication is a put-down. I am thinking of a guy who always refers to his spouse as "the wife." (I feel like greeting her by saying, "Hello, *The,* how are you?") And there are wives who are always saying no to their husbands. Those fellows can never do anything right; every story they tell is interrupted seven times: "Honey, it wasn't Tuesday; it was Wednesday. It wasn't nine o'clock; it was a quarter after. It wasn't fifty dollars; it was five hundred. You didn't win it; you lost it!"

Some children are always saying no to their parents: "You don't understand me." "You don't care." "Why can't you be like Marcia's parents?" And some parents are always saying no to their children. Perhaps we think that saying no is the way to love them, or by saying no we are helping our children become better: "Will you ever be on time?" "Aren't you ever going to grow up?" "When will you. . . ?" "Why don't you. . . ?"

Oh, we know very well how to say no!

Let's go back and think about what it means to say a loving yes. We are now in the parking lot of the church and there "he" is, driving up early. *Yes!* We are sitting down in the church pew and notice that Sister Smith is going to sing. *Yes!* The pastor gives the call to worship: "I was glad when they said unto me, let us go into the house of the Lord." *Oh, yes!* My daughter's room is messy. *Yes!* The story is not quite right. *Okay!*

Remember, saying yes to someone does not mean that you approve of or agree with everything that person does. It does not mean that your heart is not broken by the choices of lifestyle made by those you love. But it does mean that in your heart you are saying, "I love you. You are a person of infinite worth. I say yes to you because we are one." I believe that in that yes the love of God is present.

Reconsider the prayer of Jesus: ". . .that the love with which thou hast loved me may be in them, and I in them (17:26)." How did the Father love the Son? The Father said yes to Him! At his baptism: "Thou art my beloved Son: with thee I am well pleased" (Mark 1:11). At his transfiguration: "This is my beloved Son; listen to him" (Mark 9:7). And supremely at the Resurrection the Father was saying yes to Jesus!

By the same token, Jesus said yes to his Father: "My food is to do the will of him who sent me, and to accomplish his work" (John 4:34). "And the word which you hear is not mine but the Father's who sent me" (14:24). "I glorified thee on earth, having accomplished the work which thou gavest me to do" (17:4). "My Father, if it be possible, let this cup pass from me; nevertheless, not as I will, but as thou wilt" (Matt. 26:39).

The Father says yes to the Son; the Son says yes to the Father. And in the Son, the Father says yes to us! Read that marvelous verse, 2 Corinthians 1:20: "For all the promises of God find their yes in him." In Christ we have guarantee of all God's promises. Right now someone very important in your life may be saying no to you. The whole world may seem to be saying no. But in Jesus Christ, God is saying yes!

"He who did not spare his own Son but gave him up for all, will he not also give us all things with him?" (Rom. 8:32).

God is saying yes to every one of us. I think we should pass along that bit of good news, like passing the bread, for this is the crux of the matter: The Father's yes, the Son's yes, the great yes of God's promises are to find their expression in our love that says yes to each other. How exciting, scary, and wonderful it is to think about this! What if we really believed that God won't quit saying yes to us? What if we really believed in each other with a yes love that wouldn't quit? And what if we just didn't quit loving each other—no matter what?

Imagine that: Someone could make a miserable blunder and we would not quit loving him. Someone could fail and we would keep on loving him. Some insecure clown could foul up our plans and we would love him anyway. Could we in the community of believers, warmed by the wonderful yet undeserved love of God, possibly keep on loving people such as this? If there is any place like that in this world, I want to be there!

Again I hear the word of the Lord, asking, "What are you going to do about loving?" You see, we have no alternative to love. Love is commanded. Therefore, we must respond to Christ by actualizing our oneness. As we create a non-judgmental, affirming, loving atmosphere what life-changing miracles can occur! What beautiful transformation can take place when we stop saying no and start reflecting the yes of God in Jesus.

Well, are you ready to vote?

All in favor, say yes!

· · ● · ·

Father, can we really believe that you say yes to us? We know it in our heads. Help us believe it in our hearts.

Lord, to whom am I saying no? Give me the vision to see others in the light of your love for me, and give me the grace to say yes.

We thank you for your affirming yes to us. And we respond in thanks and praise with our own amen. Yes!

CHAPTER · 12

Jesus' Last Words For His Disciples

I want us to review the priestly prayer of Jesus one more time. Let us run it through our mental computer and press the button labeled *they*. We should pay close attention to the *they* verses in which Jesus talks about his disciples. By the grace of God, I am a disciple of Jesus Christ. If you are too, we should examine these verses together to see what aspirations our Lord has for us:

· "They have kept thy word" (John 17:6).

· "Now they know that everything that thou hast given me is from thee; for I have given them the words which thou gavest me, and they have received them and know in truth that I came from thee; and they have believed that thou didst send me" (v. 7).

· "They are thine" (v. 9).

· "They are in the world" (v. 11).

· "They are not of the world" (v. 16).

If I were to attempt to characterize Christian disciples, I don't know what I would write down; but in these simple statements recorded by John, Jesus has described all of us in very clear terms. When we review these statements, we can identify four basic declarations that Jesus said about us; and these may be grouped in two related pairs:

One and Two: Disciples keep Jesus' words; therefore, they know who Jesus is.

Three and Four: Disciples are in the world; but they belong to God.

We have discussed some of these ideas in earlier chapters. Now let us bring them together, beginning with statements one and two:

When I first began studying John 17, I made a list of these *they* verses; at the top of my list I simply wrote: *Disciples know who Jesus is; therefore, they keep his words.* Then I went on to the other verses. But I kept coming back to the first verses of Jesus' prayer and thinking about them. Do you know what I discovered? I found that my instinctive order of things was totally reversed. I had written: *Disciples know; therefore, they obey.* Yet that order is precisely the opposite of Jesus' prayer and of the New Testament as a whole: *Disciples obey; therefore, they know!*

We are prone to try to convince unbelievers of who Jesus is. We try to show them what he has done and what he stands for. But those who hear us perceive that our approach is doctrinal, defensive—or offensive. When I began to see the Lord's intended order, I felt a great sense of relief; because if I have to convince people of who Jesus is before I can get them to obey him, I have to be a lot smarter than they! But it's a marvelous feeling to be able to relax in the understanding that I do not have to have all the philosophical or theological answers when I tell someone about Jesus. My task is not to meet the objections and questions. In witnessing, my task is to begin at the point of obedience rather than the point of full understanding.

This has been a liberating insight into my own Christian experience. I do not have to be fully assured of who Jesus is before I come to obedience; rather, if I will obey, I will come to understand. There is simply no way to adequately communicate to you the sense of freedom this insight has brought to my life!

Listen again to Jesus: "I have given them the words which thou gavest me, and they have received them and know in truth that I came from thee; and they have *believed* that thou didst send me" (John 17:8, italics mine). The point of beginning the Christian life is the point of obedience. When Jesus first encountered the men who later followed him, they did not completely know who he was. They had some clues; they had enjoyed times of intimate fellowship with him. But they did not comprehend the full truth about Jesus. They didn't know about the shepherds, the star, the manger, or the angel. They didn't know the legends of the "other wise man," or the little drummer boy, or "Amahl and the Night Visitors." Such lovers of myth we are! But the first followers of Jesus didn't know any of these things. They simply began to follow him and listen to him. Through the days, weeks, and months they began to say yes to him.

I love to reread this line from Jesus' prayer: "I have given them the words which thou gavest me, and they have *received* them" (italics mine). *Received* is an intriguing word. Jesus' disciples *received* his teachings; they "let them in"; and consequently they came to know who he was.

One day Jesus led his disciples north to Caesarea Philippi and asked, "Who do you say that I am?" (Matt. 16:15).

Peter answered first, of course. "You are the Christ, the Son of the living God" (v. 16).

And Jesus said, "Blessed are you, Simon, Bar-Jona! For flesh and blood has not revealed this to you, but my Father who is in heaven" (v. 17).

This revelation did not come at the beginning of Peter's discipleship, but in the middle; it came as the result of weeks and months of following, responding, obeying, and listening to Jesus. Gradually there was a beautiful dawning of the truth as the Holy Spirit opened up to Peter who Jesus really was. I believe that is the pattern for us. Assurance does not begin our relationship with Christ; it comes as the result of our obedience to Christ.

Wherever you are on your spiritual journey, if you have some doubt or confusion or misunderstanding—if you are trying to decipher what's what, who's who, what's dumb and what really matters, what's cultural and what's eternal—I think the Lord has a word for you here. As you begin to obey him, you will come to growing assurance and certainty about these things.

So often we want a thrilling experience that will lift us up like the tide and set us down in a world of confident assurance. We want an "old-time gospel experience" that brings the emotion and eliminates the doubt. Of course we do. But may I repeat something I stated earlier in this book? I am learning that we don't need some great emotional experience; we've already had that. What we really need is a genuine, careful, deliberate *obedience to what we know.* So when I talk about obedience, I am not talking about things I can't understand or can't do. I am not talking about the words of Jesus that are still obscure. What bothers me are Jesus' words that are understandable and do-able. What disturbs me is that I seldom allow the words of Jesus to come down into my daily conversation, my daily patterns of thought and response—words like "Judge not," "Be not anxious," "You don't have to retaliate," "Take up your cross and follow me." I feel uncomfortable with words that tell me, "When you go to a banquet, don't go wandering around the head table looking for your name. Just go in and sit down at the end somewhere. If they want you, they'll come and get you." The worst part of Jesus' words like these is that I understand them . . . *I just understand them* . . . and don't do them.

But when we begin to obey Jesus in the little-big things of life, our assurance grows. As Elton Trueblood said, "The eyes of the soul are washed by obedience."

I do not mean to imply that all of our doubts and problems

with the Christian faith come from disobedience, just most of them. Often underneath our points of uncertainty and confusion there is a closing of the eyes or a turning away from something that we know God wants us to do. So much is solved by our simple, honest obedience to him. That is a hard word, but a good word; not only a word of judgment, but a word of hope.

I read about a young skeptic who loved to argue with a guru who lived in a hut at the top of a mountain. The skeptic said, "Father, come out. I would talk with you about my doubts."

The elderly man said, "Son, come in. I would talk with you about your sins."

Obedience is a word of hope, isn't it?

· · ● · ·

You know what Christian people say at a funeral or in the hospital: "I wonder what people do who don't know the Lord." That's what we say to each other, isn't it? Well, what *do* people do without Jesus? Think of all the lonely people in the midst of the masses. Think of how our affluent society has left deep, black chasms and aching voids in the hearts of people and how those people try to fill their chasms with so many things that don't fit. During these days of worldwide crisis and chaos, we Christians have a word. That word is the teaching of Jesus Christ, supported by the affirmation of our faith. At the heart of our world there is an anchor, a rock—a Savior. Perhaps you know this song:

> In times like these you need a Saviour;
> In times like these you need an anchor.

Be very sure, be very sure,
Your anchor holds and grips the Solid Rock!
—Ruth Caye Jones*

What a rock we have in Jesus! And that confidence in him does not belong exclusively to the few who happen to have the right personality or the right emotional experience.

Of course I thank God for those who have had "fantastic" experiences. I once talked with a fellow at college who had been wallowing in a life of sin and whose mother had been praying earnestly for him. He said he had a vision in which Jesus came and talked to him. The fellow tried to tell himself that the vision was simply an illusion; but it would not go away. It was a radical, transforming vision. He surrendered his life to Christ because of it.

That's great, but I do not know what he was talking about. I never had a vision like that, so I cannot assess such an experience. It makes no sense in terms of my own experience. I had to come to my knowledge of Jesus, not by some out-of-this-world experience, but by simple obedience. I am thinking again of the disciple who asked, "Lord, how will you manifest yourself to us, and not to the world?" Jesus replied: "If a man loves me, he will *keep my word,* and my Father will love him, and we will come to him and make our home." What astonishing simplicity I see in that!

I am thinking also of a story that I have heard all my life, from Jesus' Sermon on the Mount: "A wise man . . . built his house upon the rock and the rain fell, and the floods came, and the winds blew and beat upon that house, but it did not fall because it had been founded on the rock. And every one who hears these words of mine and does not do them will be like a foolish man who built his house upon the sand; and the rain fell, and the floods came, and beat against that house, and it fell; and great was the fall of it" (Matt. 7:24–27).

---

*"In Times Like These," copyright © 1944 Mrs. Ruth Caye Jones.

Though I have heard those words all my life, I am just beginning to understand them. The gospel song warns,

> Be very sure, be very sure,
> Your anchor holds and grips the Solid Rock.

How do we build on a rock? How do we know our lives have been made secure? What is the key to obtaining the spiritual stability that will outlast the rain, winds, and floods of life? *Hearing and doing the words of Jesus.*

· · ● · ·

These words meet me right where I am with my needs, struggles, and desires. I am sure they will continue to meet me for the rest of my life. And I care what happens to me for the rest of my life; I have no desire to die on the vine. I want to be alive and fruitful for the next twenty years (or for how many more years of life the Lord gives me). Where is newness of life for me? Shall I wait for some kind of holy vision?

What about you? Are you waiting for Jesus to come to the foot of your bed? What will be the source of certainty in your life? What will be the basis for your understanding and growth? I think I know. It is the same for you as for me. As we hear and obey *the words of Jesus,* my life will be built upon the rock —and so will yours.

Are you listening? Am I listening? Jesus surely has some words for us.

· · ● · ·

O Jesus, your words are so near to us—so easily available. Could it be that we are not really listening? Are we looking everywhere else and listening to everything else, in hopes of finding what we need?

Quiet us so that we can hear you. Open our hearts to your life-giving words. They are beautiful, wonderful words and we really do need to listen. Amen.

DISCUSSION QUESTIONS

Introduction

1. The author says, "I once read that in these comments [i.e., the Farewell Discourse] we find everything that is most precious to our Christian heritage: every gift, every promise, every commandment, every warning, every resource that the living Christ has given to those who love him in sincerity and truth." Scan the entire Farewell Discourse (John 13:31–17:26) and list what you find, along with the appropriate Scripture reference:

Gifts   *Reference*

Promises   *Reference*

Commandments   *Reference*

Warnings   *Reference*

2. Read Ephesians 4:7–8, 11–13. According to these verses, what was Jesus' *purpose* in giving these things to his church when he returned to heaven?

3. "We should remember that the eleven men with Jesus that night [i.e., at the Last Supper] represent *the church*." In what ways do they represent us?

4. Some Bible scholars feel that the Gospel accounts of Jesus' ministry have been distorted—even falsified— because they were written several years after Jesus' death and resurrection. Does the author agree with this view? What does he think is the effect of this lapse of time between the event and the writing?

5. What is the difference between *hearing* and *listening*?

6. Why does the author say, "Christians like you and me do not take the words of Jesus as seriously as we ought"?

Cite some evidence of what he means—examples from your own life or the lives of Christians that you know:

7. ". . .The theology of the whole Bible is essentially a theology of the Word." How might the Bible be different if it were based on a theology of *feeling* or a theology of *attitude?*

8. Dr. Welch emphasizes that Jesus' speaking and our listening "are vital to the relationship we have with the Lord." In what ways is this transaction *vital* (literally, life-giving)?

Explain how this relationship would begin to die if Christ did not speak or we did not listen:

9. List some areas of your life in which you need to hear what the Lord is saying to you now:

10. List some areas in which you hear what Jesus is saying, but you are refusing to do what he says:

Chapter 1

1. What are some of the questions you want to ask Jesus?

   Do these questions ever interrupt your prayers? What happens?

2. Recall some times you failed the Lord. Briefly describe how you failed him:

   Why did you fail him in these situations?

3. Dr. Welch says that many of our failures begin with our not trusting the Lord to supply our needs. In the situations you have described, do you see any evidence of weak faith?

4. Jesus call us to believe in him. For each situation you described under question 2, write a statement of faith that begins: "If I believed in Jesus, I would. . . ." Complete the statement by describing what you would do in that situation if you had faith in Christ.

5. What are some things Jesus could accomplish by leaving his disciples that he could not have accomplished if he stayed with them and died a natural death?

6. Do you think we are nearer Christ's return than we are to his going away? Why?

   How is your life affected by the prospect of Christ's return? Do you live any differently because you expect him to return?

7. Dr. Welch notes that Jesus' words of farewell are bathed in a mood of victory. How might you reflect Jesus' victory in your family life?

in your business dealings?

in your worship with other Christians?

8. List some areas of life in which you feel defeated (or discouraged):

9. Talk with the Lord in prayer. Commit these defeats to him; claim his victory over them.

10. Read 1 Corinthians 15:54–58. Rephrase it in your own words:

Chapter 2

1. What are some other "ways to God" that various cults and popular leaders propose in the place of Jesus?

2. Dr. Welch says, "Jesus is the true way to the Father because (1) he reveals to us the truth about the Father and (2) he shares with us the life of the Father." Explain in your own words what Jesus reveals about God:

   How does Jesus give us access to the life of the Father?

3. Some unbelievers recoil from Jesus' statement that "no one comes to the Father but by me." They feel there are many different ways to find peace with God. They believe we are being too narrow-minded when we insist that Jesus is the only way to be delivered from sin and

113

death. What would you say to a non-Christian friend who expressed such feelings to you?

4. "We can't search for God and find him for ourselves. . . . God makes himself known to us." In what ways is God making himself known to you today?

5. Explain the difference between saying (a) Jesus is the one who points the way to God and (b) Jesus is the way to God:

6. What difficulties will you be able to face more confidently today because you know Christ is with you?

Chapter 3

1. Explain in your own words the difference between "knowing about God" and "knowing God."

2. In what ways will a person's life be changed by knowing God?

3. Dr. Welch reminds us of the distorted views of God that many people receive during their childhood years. What can Christian parents do to make sure their children have a right understanding of God?

   In what ways can Christian parents act as valid models of God's love?

4. Read Colossians 3:18–22 and discuss it with a Christian friend. Discuss your own place in a family. In light of this Scripture, how well are you fulfilling your role in the family?

5. Because of the widespread fuzzy thinking about God, we have often developed some strange notions about life and death. Dr. Welch describes one example of this: the funeral oration that suggests God snatches little children for himself. List some other strange ideas that you have heard, based on fuzzy thinking about who God is:

6. Jesus reveals what God is like. Describe the character and manner of Jesus, based on what you already know from reading the Gospels:

Do you believe these characteristics of Jesus the Son are also true of God the Father? Why or why not?

7. List some other words that you think describe the nature and activity of God:

Chapter 4

1. Thomas is often called the "doubting disciple" because he would not believe Jesus had risen from the dead until he touched Jesus' scars for himself. At the beginning of this chapter, we see Thomas in another doubting, questioning role as he asks how the resurrected Jesus will manifest himself to his followers and not to the world. Would you say that Thomas' doubting is healthy or not healthy?

What is the difference between destructive doubt and healthy doubt?

How can doubting help a Christian grow?

2. Recall an event in your life when God seemed most real to you:

3. What did you learn about God in that experience?

4. Dr. Welch says, ". . .We must let the words of Jesus seep into the attitudes, responses, and decisions of daily life. In this process, our heavenly Father makes himself known to us in loving intimacy. We can know God the Father both in precept and in person; and the key to this knowledge is *obedience*." Recall an experience in which you were reluctant to obey God:

Why were you reluctant to obey him?

What did you learn about God through your obedience (or your disobedience) in that situation?

5. Jesus promises that he and his Father "will come and make our home with" anyone who obeys. Do you believe the Lord is "at home" with you right now? Why or why not?

6. If you are estranged from God, what steps of obedience is he calling you to take?

7. Make a covenant of obedience with God. Write in the space below the next step of obedience that you plan to take in order to show your love for him:

Chapter 5

1. Read some Old Testament passages that describe Israel as the "vine" that God planted (Ps. 80; Jer. 2:20–22; Hos. 10:1–2). What do these Scriptures reveal about Israel's relationship with God?

2. Reread John 14:1–5. What will God do with the unfruitful branches of his spiritual vine?

3. Who are these branches?

   Apply this Scripture to your own life; how should it affect the way you live?

4. What are some specific kinds of fruit that God expects from a Christian?

5. What are some ways in which God may "prune" an unfruitful Christian?

Recall a "pruning" experience from your own Christian life:

6. *Pruning* implies pain. But according to Dr. Welch, what else does it imply? What are some beneficial results of spiritual pruning?

7. Meditate on Jesus' promise, "Ask whatever you will. . . ." If you were to ask God the most pressing desire of your heart right now, what would it be?

Submit this request to God. Let him evaluate it. Does God reveal anything about your desire that is unworthy of him or contradictory to his will?

8. Examine your own spiritual "staying power." What are some things that tempt you to drift away from the Lord?

What are some pressures that make obedience difficult for you?

9. What promises of God can you claim when you feel yourself slipping out of your place in the vine? Write some Scripture promises that reassure you:

Chapter 6

1. Dr. Welch comments that many Christians have "neutral or negative feelings about the Holy Spirit." What sort of feelings do you have when you enter a study of the Spirit? Why?

2. What questions do you have about the Holy Spirit and his work?

3. List the Holy Spirit's official titles mentioned in the Scripture passages that you have studied in this chapter:

Which of these best describes the Spirit's role in your life? Why?

4. "...We have tended to be tritheists instead of trinitarians," Welch says. "What I mean is, at the practical level we believe in three Gods, side by side, instead of one God whose nature is to be a fellowship of three persons." What affect does this belief have on a Christian's prayer?

worship?

witnessing?

general attitude toward God?

5. The tritheist view of God leads to a threefold division of the Bible, too; each person of the Godhead is supposed to be represented by a different section of Scripture. If this were true, how would it affect our understanding of biblical inspiration and authority? Would it mean that modern Christians should hold some portions of Scripture in higher regard than others? Why?

6. Notice Dr. Welch's suggestion for reading the New Testament in the order in which the books probably were written: (1) Paul's epistles, (2) the Gospels, (3) the General Epistles beginning with Hebrews, (4) the Book of Acts, and (5) the Book of Revelation. What might be some benefits of reading the New Testament in this order?

7. "The Holy Spirit continues his guiding ministry today, and the words of Jesus are his instruments of guidance." What procedure might you follow to seek the Spirit's guidance for a personal decision, using the words of Jesus? List the steps:

8. The Bible warns us to "test the spirits to see whether they are from God, because many false prophets have gone out into the world" (1 John 4:1b). How might you test some guidance that you think came from the Holy Spirit to make sure it did not come from an ungodly spirit instead?

9. Write your own prayer concerning the Holy Spirit. Mention specific needs you have today in which the Spirit could give you comfort, guidance, and greater exaltation of Christ.

Chapter 7

1. Read Hebrews 8:1–6, which describes Jesus' priestly ministry in detail. What priestly function did he fulfill when he offered the prayer of John 17?

In what ways did Jesus prove that he was faithful to his calling?

List what Jesus requests for his followers in this prayer:

2. In what respect is Jesus' priestly ministry better than the ministry of the Old Testament priests?

3. "...A biblical name was not just a label of identification; it expressed the essential character of the person who bore the name." What does Matthew 1:21–23 tell us about the names (and character) of Jesus?

4. What do you think the third commandment means when it says, "You shall not misuse the name of the Lord your God..." ("shalt not take the name of the Lord thy God in vain," KJV)? cursing? false swearing? lying under oath? something else? Explain your answer.

5. What kind of relationship does God expect to have with us if he is willing to tell us his name?

6. Meditate upon the various meanings of *Yahweh*. This word reveals much about the character of God. What are some things that it implies about God's relationship with you?

7. "Jesus came not only *knowing* the name of God but *bearing* the name of God. He became the ultimate revelation of God to his people. . . . He fulfilled the promise of God's presence; he became the place where we meet God." Since we are to be Christlike, what are some ways we can "bear the name of God" in our daily lives?

Chapter 8

1. List some "glorious people" that you know:

List some "glorious experiences" you have had:

Based on these two lists, what would you say the word *glory* means to you?

2. Dr. Welch says, "If my glory rests in something that I can do, I will be greatly disturbed when I meet someone who can do it better. If my glory depends on the people I know, then I am vulnerable to depression when those people let me down." Recall a situation in which your "glory" was deflated because someone was able to outshine your ability:

Recall a situation in which your "glory" was deflated because an impressive friend let you down:

How did these experiences change your estimate of your own "glory"?

3. Welch warns of "a subtle shift in attitude from total dependence upon God to dependence upon the [spiritual] gift." Which spiritual gifts do you have?

Have you ever been tempted to trust your gifts more than you trust God himself? If so, how did you discover the shift had occurred?

4. What is the basic source of your feelings of self-worth? job? family? possessions? or something else?

How can you tell?

5. What do you think Dr. Welch means when he says we must "take our gifts and talents to the cross"?

6. What are some personal "glories" that you should surrender to Christ?

Chapter 9

1. What do you think Dr. Welch means by being "fully present" to someone else?

2. In what ways are you "fully present" to God?

   In what respects are you a "missing person," so far as God is concerned?

3. How are you "fully present" to the world around you?

   Would you say you are more "present" to your world than you are to God? Explain your answer.

4. Some Christians try to escape from the world to express God's full ownership of their lives. Do you see any potential problems in this?

5. What are some benefits of occasional retreats and devotional times of solitude?

6. Explain how you think Jesus expects you to live as an "in-the-world" Christian. How does his prayer affect your lifestyle, your mental outlook, and your relationships with others?

7. Dr. Welch offers this definition of *holiness*: "To be holy means to be different by virtue of belonging to God." What are some ways in which a holy person should be different from an ungodly person? (Be sure to compare your answers with those of another Christian. You may be surprised at how much your views of holy living disagree!)

8. In simpler terms, Dr. Welch says that a holy person is a "Christ-person." How does someone become a Christ-person, one whose life is fully devoted to God? (Describe the steps of consecration to God, as you understand them.)

9. The author speaks of a "radical belonging to God" and a "growing likeness to Jesus." In what sense is this an instantaneous experience? In what sense is it a progressive one?

10. Dr. Welch says, "At the very core of the matter, holiness means God-centeredness, Christlikeness, and God-sentness." Briefly describe how your own life reflects each of these qualities. How can anyone tell that your life is God-centered?

Christlike?

God-sent?

Chapter 10

1. What evidences of Christian disunity do you see?

2. How does this disunity affect unbelievers' attitudes toward the gospel?

3. Some argue that unity would cause them to compromise their convictions; they fear they would have to surrender their cherished beliefs to fall in line with other Christians. But is Christian *unity* the same as Christian *uniformity*? Explain your answer.

Does church *unity* require *uniformity*? Again explain your answer.

4. Dr. Welch's illustration of the extended communion table suggests that all Christians have one thing in common: the shared life of Jesus Christ. What are some practical ways that Christians from different denominations (even different congregations in the same denomination) show the world what they have in common?

5. "I am chagrined at the petty things that divide us," Dr. Welch says, "when in truth the oneness we have in Christ is the great reality of the Christian life." Have you ever been embarrassed by a display of Christian

division or hostility? If so, briefly describe what happened:

How might this problem have been prevented?

6. List three of your Christian neighbors who are somewhat different from you:

What makes them different?

What are some specific things you can do to express your oneness with them, despite your differences?

7. List some specific things your congregation might do to promote a sense of unity among its people (then share this list with your pastor):

8. How might your congregation express its oneness with some other Christian groups in your community, even though deep differences divide you?

9. How would Christian unity, more openly expressed, affect unbelievers' attitudes toward Christ and the gospel?

Chapter 11

1. In order to give us a compact definition of love, Dr. Welch begins with the oneness that Christians have in Christ (the theme of the previous chapter), explaining that *love* is the outward expression of our oneness: "Love is our felt oneness behaviorized, actualized in practice, and manifested in discernible acts of Christlike caring." Give some examples of what you think he means.

Love is Christian oneness "behaviorized." Examples:

Love is Christian oneness "actualized in practice." Examples:

Love is Christian oneness "manifested in discernible acts of Christlike caring." Examples:

2. Why do you suppose we human beings are so accustomed to saying no? What are we trying to accomplish by saying no to other people?

3. Dr. Welch points out that God says an affirming "yes!" to each one of us. What are some ways in which God expresses his "yes" to you?

4. Notice how Dr. Welch describes the results of affirming other people in the spirit of God's affirming yes: "Someone could make a miserable blunder and we would not quit loving him. Someone could fail and we would keep on loving him. Some insecure clown could foul up our plans and we would love him anyway." Who has done such things in your life recently? (Remember, each one provides you an opportunity to say God's yes!)

5. Often we suppose that love is an emotion we express when we "feel like it." But Dr. Welch explains that love is commanded. It is a direct mandate from our Lord, whether we feel like loving or not. What Scriptural evidence does he give for this?

6. How might you act differently today if you were always conscious of God's love-command? (If you are stumped by this question, picture someone you will meet who is difficult to love; describe how you might say an affirming yes to that person.)

Chapter 12

1. Write out the "they" passages from John 17 quoted at the beginning of this chapter; in each case, substitute your own name for the word *they*:

Are these statements true? If not, what things in your life should change in order to make them true?

2. Consider the personal implications of this truth: *Disciples obey; therefore, they know.* Are there some aspects of God's will that you seem unable to know?

Are there some aspects of God's will that you are failing to obey?

According to the principle stated above, how would your *obedience* to God affect your *knowledge* of his will?

3. Dr. Welch points out that Jesus' first disciples knew nothing about his miraculous birth because the Gospels had not been written and the truth of Christmas had not been publicly proclaimed. In fact, his first disciples did not know much about Jesus; yet they heard his commands, obeyed them, and learned more about him as a result of obeying. What does a person need to know in order to become a Christian?

How should this affect your witnessing to unbelievers?

4. Why does Dr. Welch say, "Obedience is a word of hope. . ."? What hope do we gain by obeying the Lord?

5. What causes the natural human heart to resent the idea of obedience?

6. Welch closes this book by suggesting that the key to obtaining spiritual stability is simply this: "Hearing and doing the words of Jesus." What might you do to *hear* Jesus' words more attentively?

How might you *do* the words of Jesus more faithfully?